The Clinical Thinking o

Wilfred Bion (1897–1979) is considered a provocative and illuminating contributor to the debate on the nature of psycho-analysis. His understanding of the processes involved constitutes a radical departure from all conceptualizations which preceded him.

In a move to recognize the importance of Bion's revolutionary thinking, Joan and Neville Symington define his contribution not in terms of a theory, but as a descriptive analysis. They locate difficulties in understanding Bion's work within the conflicting theories and preoccupations which readers naturally bring with them and which they encourage the reader to set aside.

The Clinical Thinking of Wilfred Bion concentrates on key concepts such as the Grid in relation to clinical practice. Each chapter examines an important theme and describes the part it has to play in Bion's revolutionary model of the mind.

This book aims to define the ground-breaking nature of Bion's work and make it accessible to both clinicians and anyone who wishes to understand the main contours of his thinking.

Joan and Neville Symington are psychoanalysts in private practice, Sydney, Australia.

The Makers of Modern Psychotherapy
Series editor: Laurence Spurling

This series of introductory, critical texts looks at the work and thought of key contributors to the development of psychodynamic psychotherapy. Each book shows how the theories examined affect clinical practice, and includes biographical material as well as a comprehensive bibliography of the contributor's work.

The field of psychodynamic psychotherapy is today more fertile but also more diverse than ever before. Competing schools have been set up, rival theories and clinical ideas circulate. These different and sometimes competing strains are held together by a canon of fundamental concepts, guiding assumptions and principles of practice.

This canon has a history, and the way we now understand and use the ideas that frame our thinking and practice is palpably marked by how they came down to us, by the temperament and experiences of their authors, the particular puzzles they wanted to solve and the contexts in which they worked. These are the makers of modern psychotherapy. Yet despite their influence, the work and life of some of these eminent figures is not well known. Others are more familiar, but their particular contribution is open to reassessment. In studying these figures and their work, this series will articulate those ideas and ways of thinking that practitioners and thinkers within the psychodynamic tradition continue to find persuasive.

Also in this series:

John Bowlby and Attachment Theory Jeremy Holmes

Frances Tustin Sheila Spensley

Heinz Kohut Allen Siegel

Forthcoming title:

R.D. Laing Zbigniew Kotowicz

The Clinical Thinking of Wilfred Bion

Joan and Neville Symington

Brunner-Routledge
Taylor & Francis Group

HOVE AND NEW YORK

First published 1996
by Routledge
11 New Fetter Lane, London EC4P 4EE

Simultaneously published in the USA and Canada
by Routledge
29 West 35th Street, New York, NY 10001

Reprinted 1997 and 1999

Reprinted 2001
by Brunner-Routledge
27 Church Road, Hove, East Sussex, BN3 2FA
325 Chestnut Street, Suite 800, Philadelphia, PA 19106

Reprinted 2003
by Brunner-Routledge
27 Church Road, Hove, East Sussex, BN3 2FA
29 West 35th Street, New York, NY 10001

Brunner-Routledge is an imprint of the Taylor & Francis Group

© 1996 Joan and Neville Symington

Typeset in Times by
Florencetype Ltd, Stoodleigh, Devon
Printed and bound in the United Kingdom by
TJ International Ltd., Padstow, Cornwall

British Library Cataloguing in Publication Data
A catalogue record for this book is available from the British Library

Library of Congress Cataloging in Publication Data
Symington, Joan, 1939–
The clinical thinking of Wilfred Bion/Joan and Neville
Symington
   p. cm. - (Makers of modern psychotherapy)
   Includes bibliographical references and index.
1. Bion, Wilfred R. (Wilfred Ruprecht), 1897-1979.
2. Psychoanalysis, 3. Psychodynamic psychotherapy.
I. Symington, Neville. II. Title. III. Series.
RC438.6.B54S96 1996
616.89' 17-dc20

ISBN 0–415–09352–X (hbk)
ISBN 0–415–09353–8 (pbk)

For Andrew and David

Contents

Acknowledgements

In struggling to grasp and understand the thinking of Wilfred Bion we have sought the advice and help of a number of colleagues and friends. There are four people whom we should like to thank in particular: Bill Stewart, Sydney Klein, Bob Gosling and Francesca Bion. Bill, an Australian philosopher, has taken a special interest in our project and has gone to the trouble to write us long letters and to put Bion into a philosophical context, which has been invaluable. Sydney Klein has given great encouragement to persevere in investigating our ideas when they have been opposed or challenged. His independence from group pressures and ability to see the special contribution of Bion in contemporary analytic theory has been a source of inspiration to us. It is particularly valuable to be able to be informed by one of Bion's analysands. Bob Gosling was most generous to us in his willingness to impart information about his experience of being in analysis with Bion, which gave us an understanding of Bion not available elsewhere. Francesca Bion met with one of us, gave freely of information about her late husband and continued to send us material which she thought would be of interest.

We also want to thank Elliott Jaques, who clarifed for us Melanie Klein's attitude to philosophy and religion; Willie McIntyre, who threw light on aspects of Bion which had not occurred to us; Isabel Menzies-Lyth – another analysand – who told us of her experiences in a group conducted by Bion; Isca Wittenberg and Frances Tustin who both gave us generous accounts of their experiences of being analysed by Bion; Albert Mason, who recounted several anecdotes and let us have his own writing on Bion; and Edwina Welham, who commissioned us to write this book and who waited patiently for our manuscript to arrive.

Lastly we would like to thank Bion himself. We had the good fortune to attend several of his workshops at the Tavistock and also at the Institute of Psycho-Analysis and were inspired by the depth of his mind and the clarity of his expression. He has enriched our understanding very considerably. We hope in this book that we can pass on a small portion of it.

The list of 'Publications by Wilfred Bion' was first published in Bion's *Cogitations*, London: H. Karnac (Books) Ltd, 1992, pp. 381–4 and is reprinted here, with amendments, by kind permission of the publishers. The extract from the 'The Thought-Fox' by Ted Hughes is reproduced from *The Hawk in the Rain* by kind permission of Faber & Faber Ltd.

Preface

We all desire to exist, said Bion in a seminar. Life, said Bergson, is the tendency to act on matter. Human beings have evolved from apes, apes from monkeys, monkeys as a branch of mammals, mammals from reptiles and so on. Evolution marks the path along which the *élan vital* has travelled in its journey. Human beings are not the finished product; the *élan vital* is still in process. When we have demonstrated the pathway, we have not explained life itself. The pathway has an identity in virtue of a chain of causal connections, but these do not tell us about life itself. Life thrusts we know not where.

In our inquiry into Bion's thinking, we desire to be faithful to his mode of investigation. Therefore, our mode of thinking about him will not follow a causal line. We wish to grasp the thinking itself and not the pathway along which he arrived at it. You cannot see life itself but you can see manifestations of it. A man fell off his horse, which then rolled on him and he lay motionless on the ground. People gathered around and said he was dead, but he just managed to raise his little finger, which was a signal large enough to tell the bystanders that he was alive. The rising finger was a manifestation of life, not life itself.

Our method, then, is to take themes, each of which is a manifestation of Bion's thought but not the thing-in-itself. Each manifestation bears a connection with another which is not causal but interdependent. We can explain things as best we can, clear away as much rubbish as we can, point to those manifestations which seem most crucial, but only you, the reader, can grasp the thought itself – life's representation.

We believe that this method is faithful to what is central to Bion, in that he was concerned to comprehend the life of the mind itself. This is in contrast to those analytical schools of thought whose focus has been upon pathological processes, diverting attention thereby from the mind's own life.

We have decided on this rather than following the chronological development of his ideas. This would have required scholarly research for which we have neither the time nor the ability. We are aiming this book at the educated reader who wants to understand the main contours of Bion's thinking, rather than the specialist. We hope also that this approach will be of practical help to clinicians. This book is different from that of Bleandonu (1994) in that all attention is geared to understanding in detail Bion's clinical theory. Bleandonu's book is biographical and sets Bion's epistemology into its philosophical context. We have concentrated on understanding Bion's concepts in relation to clinical practice. Our book is especially for the clinician who is trying to see the application of Bion's thinking to his or her own work with patients. A serious student of Bion would need to read both books; they complement each other. This book will not absolve the reader from hard thinking.

Psychoanalysis seen through Bion's eyes is a radical departure from all conceptualizations which preceded him. We have not the slightest hesitation in saying that he is the deepest thinker within psychoanalysis – and this statement does not exclude Freud. If the reader registers no shock, if she is not flabbergasted to realize that all she has understood is now in the balance, if she does not gasp in horror to realize that she has to start all over again, then we have failed dismally in our task and the book will have been a failure.

The structure of the book

Bion's mature thinking developed between 1953 and 1967. In those fourteen years he wrote eight papers and three books. In that time he reached a climax of understanding. *Attention and Interpretation* (1970), *Brazilian Lectures* (1990), *A Memoir of the Future* (1991) and many other lectures and workshops in the New World and England (on his frequent visits in his last years) are all elaborations of the insights gained in this crucial period and are the logical if imaginative outcome of his central understanding. In the work on groups, moreover, one can see the first fore-shadowing of his mature theory. The schema around which his mature thinking is symbolized and structured is the Grid. Conceptually, therefore, we have placed the Grid at the centre and we radiate out from it and back to it. Many people throw up their hands when confronted with the Grid. The work of trying to understand it will more than repay the effort, however. Those who make a sustained effort to understand the Grid will have a good chance of grasping Bion's thinking at its centre. In the attempt to elucidate his central comprehension of the analytic process we shall illustrate some aspects from his later works but we do not devote a specific chapter to it.

Bion formulated and condensed his thinking into the Grid. The structure of the book therefore reflects our attempt to elucidate it. Some chapters are direct expositions of aspects of it, but even others which may seem more remote from it can be seen in relation to it and to receive illumination from it. So, for instance, Chapter 2 on the character of Bion becomes comprehensible in a new way in the light of the Grid. His character reflects his belief that the only way of knowing psychic reality is through intuiting it and of knowing O by *becoming* it, which is reflected in the simplicity in his character. His theory of the proto-mental system in his book *Experiences in Groups* (1961) foreshadows his more mature conceptualization of beta elements. The Grid, we believe, is therefore central to any understanding of Bion and it is for this reason that we have structured the book in this way. In our last chapter we try to demonstrate the unity of structure in Bion's thinking. Such a unity is the hall-mark of a great thinker. In that unity there is a disarming simplicity in which there is a great depth.

	Definitory hypotheses 1	ψ 2	Notation 3	Attention 4	Inquiry 5	Action 6	...n.
A β-elements	A1	A2				A6	
B α-elements	B1	B2	B3	B4	B5	B6	...Bn
C Dream thoughts, dreams, myths	C1	C2	C3	C4	C5	C6	...Cn
D Pre-conception	D1	D2	D3	D4	D5	D6	...Dn
E Conception	E1	E2	E3	E4	E5	E6	...En
F Concept	F1	F2	F3	F4	F5	F6	...Fn
G Scientific deductive system		G2					
H Algebraic calculus							

The Grid

Chapter 1

The theoretical disjunction between Bion and Freud/Klein

Insight into truth is the flash which in live conversation upon serious matters carries one beyond words.

(Murdoch 1992: 174)

Bion said that to be without memory or desire is the mental state which prepares the analyst best for the forthcoming clinical session. We believe that to understand Bion it is necessary to adopt the same attitude of mind. Most analysts come to Bion assuming that he follows Freud's and Klein's model of the mind, but this is a mistaken assumption that blocks understanding of his insight into the life of the mind.

A Catholic priest told us this story about himself. As a child he had been told that baptism was a sacrament which washes original sin from the soul. At theological college he unlearned this definition and replaced it with one which conceptualized baptism as inner commitment to a new way of living. With the oil of ordination hardly dry on his hands he set off to teach a class of schoolchildren the meaning of baptism. At the start of the class he asked them all a question – 'What is baptism?' They all answered in chorus: 'BAPTISM IS A SACRAMENT WHICH WASHES THE STAIN OF ORIGINAL SIN FROM THE SOUL.' The priest then told them that this definition was not correct and he would now devote the class to explaining what baptism was. He explained how baptists were baptized, how the early Christians went down into the waters in white garments symbolizing death to old ways and rising up with new life and commitment to God and fellow human beings. He explained that baptism was a new birth, that it was not a washing away of sin but the beginning of new life. In his enthusiasm he displayed photographs and explained the whole ceremony in what he believed was an interesting way. He also tried to show how baptism was a sort of conversion of the heart to a new vision of life. At the end of the class he asked the pupils 'What is baptism?' They all answered in chorus: 'BAPTISM IS A SACRAMENT WHICH WASHES THE STAIN OF ORIGINAL SIN FROM THE SOUL.'

A model or theory in the mind can obstruct learning. We believe that those most familiar with the theories of psychoanalysis are those most likely not to learn what Bion has to offer. They are like those schoolchildren whom the priest was trying to teach. We have no reason to believe that our effort to teach the thought of Bion to those in the mental health field will be any more successful than that of the Catholic priest. Just like those children we have deeply rooted assumptions that blind us to reality and unfortunately training analysts frequently inculcate their own view very firmly into the patient.

In order to paint a subject it is necessary to ditch a lot of mental assumptions. I may look and know that the table in front of me is separate from the book-case against which it rests but visually it may be the same – there is no distinction between them. Therefore in order to paint the scene in front of me I have to unlearn what I know in order to see it. Similarly, when asked I may say that a wall in front of me is white, whereas in fact it displays many shades of colour through shadows and refracted light. If I look closely there may be no part of the wall that is white at all.

Bion's starting point is the phenomenology of the analytic session itself. He examines the session and its constituent elements. These elements include the emotional atmosphere, the feeling of the session, the analyst's emotional state and his thoughts, feelings and desires. The focus of the investigation is upon the inner processes of the mind. We cannot emphasize enough that Bion's starting points are the phenomena encountered in the analytic session. In order to explicate these phenomena he uses concepts from philosophy, mathematics and psychoanalysis in the same way as we use language to convey an experience, but it is the experience itself that he is trying to elucidate. Bion describes the phenomena, making use of theories in order to do so. He uses theories, models and myths as a language to describe the activity of the mind. What Bion provides, then, is not a theory but a descriptive analysis or a descriptive synthesis.

This analysis of the phenomenology had to be conducted according to some principles; those which Bion selects are the emergence of truth and mental growth. The mind grows through exposure to truth. Bion investigates the process through which truth evolves and the process through which truth is blocked. This is the foundation and it is the *only* assumption that Bion makes. He analyses all processes with these two co-ordinates as his basic assumption. Theories that he employs are used to represent stages in these processes; they are never used as the basic orientation upon which the rest is built. Therefore any use of theory is always a provisional means of representing a stage in the development or degeneration of truth. What follows in this chapter is an attempt to clear the mind of those theories that occupy so large a position within psychoanalysis.

Freud was what philosophers term a hard determinist. This means that an event must always be explained by an efficient impersonal cause. So, for instance, Freud theorized that a symptom arises because the sexual drive has been dammed up and found a substitute satisfaction in the symptom; so the symptom is caused by the damming up of the sexual drive. In Bion's conceptualization there is no such causal connection. A patient entered analysis because he suffered from asthma and believed that psychological factors underlay it.[1] This was the articulated reason that brought him to analysis; the real reason, however, was just as real but much more difficult to define. Another patient wanted to train to be an analyst and requested analysis because it was a condition of training. Yet another patient sought analysis because of obsessional symptoms that obstructed his capacity to work. In each of these cases the analysis was slave to a defined objective which was quite describable in a straightforward way. In all these cases these were the symptoms and the internal difficulty for which these patients wanted treatment had not been defined. It is as if the patients had come to the analyst and said, 'I want an analysis but I do not know why.'

The analysis reveals the inner situation which constitutes the problem. The symptom then is the cover-story for the analysis. It sounds all right if I say: 'I am having analysis for my asthma', or: 'I am having analysis because I want to train as an analyst',

---

[1] Unless specified otherwise, case study examples are drawn from our own clinical experience.

or: 'I am having analysis because I was depressed after my marriage broke down.' This sounds more respectable than saying: 'I am having analysis because I am not able to think', or: 'I am having analysis because I have spent my life deceiving myself', or: 'I am having analysis because I have made a fuck-up of my life.'

The analysis is the diagnosis of the inner truth. The patient with asthma displayed the following attitudes which were connected with it: he withheld information about himself from the analyst, he had black moods which drove his wife to the edge of despair, he was in a constant rush, he poured out language from which thought was absent, he demanded that the analysis cure the asthma within two years. Now what underlay these symptoms was not a dammed-up sexual drive but a diabolical spitefulness which he hid from himself. All we can be certain of is that the asthma, the obsessional symptoms or the desire to be an analyst is not it. Underlying this is a view that the symptom is 'caused' by a specific something rather than a cover-up for the real reason. No patient has ever come to us in a consultation and said, 'I have come for analysis because I am unable to love.' The patient comes with a cover-story instead: 'I have asthma and I have begun to think that there may be psychological reasons behind it.' So the symptom is a cover for the truth. It is also a hidden sign of the truth for the patient. The idea that it is because of a dammed-up sexual drive fits with a physicalist anthroposophy. This kind of causal explanation, said Bion, rationalizes a sense of persecution. It's as if I say, 'All my troubles are due to the fact that my mother was depressed after I was born', or: 'My asthma is because my sexual drive is all dammed up', or 'All my troubles are because . . .'

Whatever the reason – and it does not really matter what it is – it justifies an inner sense of persecution. Therefore the supposed cause is part of a paranoid constellation. Bion says that this persecution is denied in order to evade a depression which the individual dreads. A patient who, as soon as a piece of behaviour became evident, immediately demanded the reason for it from the analyst did so to fend off a depression which threatened to overwhelm him. When a person realizes how persecuted he is and the illusory nature of this, he often becomes very depressed.

We try to draw this out with a clinical example. The patient is a woman who hated her father. Apparently he accused her of things that she had not done, was rude and vulgar, and created scenes in the home. This 'caused' her to leave home as soon as she could, carve out a career for herself as a lawyer, putting no demands, financial or otherwise, upon her father. She married when she was 21. She had eczema, bronchitis and frequent bouts of coughing. She came to analysis because after she had tried a medicine chest of remedies her GP suggested to her that her condition might be psychologically based. On undergoing analysis she found breaks in treatment either at weekends or during holidays panic-making and she had bouts of *tussis nervosa* as soon as the analyst went away. In his absence he existed in her mind as an object fixed in the consulting-room, and she knew for certain that she did not exist in his mind. The tie between her and the analyst was felt by her to be physical and not mental and this was strengthened when he gave her extra sessions at weekends and during breaks in the early stages of treatment. She would often sit eating on a park bench near our London home. The interpretation that she was a baby clinging desperately to Mummy – holding onto her physically – made sense to her. 'When the session ends and I push you out the door – out of the bedroom – little Mary is not going to be beaten and stays on Mummy's lap [bench].' This interpretation also enraged her because she hated the analyst being able to see the child in her. She believed she was a mature and independent woman.

Now these factors – a physical clinging to the analyst, inwardly tortured by believing that the analyst would seduce her sexually; an idealization of the analyst; an inner omnipotence; an indignant self-righteousness; the eruption of eczema; the absence of mental representation for outer figures and the consequent absence of a capacity for thinking – are all elements in an emotional constellation. It is part of psychoanalytical experience that it only becomes possible to understand an emotional constellation when it begins to cede to a different pattern. Now in this patient a different pattern did emerge. Its constituents were as follows: a de-idealization (seeing the analyst as a person who made mistakes); a confidence that the analyst would not seduce her; an image of the analyst as a person existing with others; a substitution of humility for omnipotence; a capacity to accept responsibility for 'bad' things that had happened between herself and others; a significant decrease in asthma attacks and a diminution of eczema; a mental representation of the analyst and the development of a capacity to think. In the light of this new pattern she sees that her previous perceptual system was distorted. However, in her new emotional constellation she becomes aware of realities which did not burden her before: regret that she had governed her life to date on these false perceptions; guilt about the way in which she had treated her husband, father and mother; sadness that she had been cut off from several avenues of 'possibility'. She had to bear personal regret, guilt and sadness. She was stuck in the first emotional constellation, feeling unable to bear these 'dark' emotions. This suggests some inner sense of their presence. There is here the emergence of truth and with it a dawning of hope. The change occurs in a decision to face pain rather than evade it. The analyst can witness a patient changing from evading pain to facing it but not the reason for doing so.

We trust that these examples will help to elucidate the factors that operate in the inner life of the individual and that these factors are not compatible with drives or instincts conceptualized as impersonal forces that *cause* this condition or that symptom.

The phenomenon of someone moving from evading pain to acceptance of suffering is in direct opposition to the pleasure principle. Yet this movement is quite central to Bion's theory of development so we have to ditch the pleasure principle and its derivatives. He says that the crucial determinant in mental growth is whether the individual 'decides' to evade frustration or to tolerate it. In the psychoanalytic process the analyst makes interpretations concerning inner pain, regret, shame, guilt or depression. Such interpretations move the patient from evasion towards acceptance of these realities. The theory that lies behind such a procedure is that acceptance of these inner realities promotes mental growth. Such an acceptance cannot be explained within the parameters of Freud's hedonistic theory. Freud explained such human behaviour on the basis of delayed gratification, that is that a present pleasure was renounced in favour of a greater quantum of pleasure at a future date. This implies the capacity to opt against pleasure at the present and the intervention of a judgement that it is better to renounce this present pleasure, with the further implication that the individual's action is not explicable by efficient causality but by a judgement motivated by desire for a future good. However, Bion implies that there is a shift from one motivational category – that determined by desire for pleasure and avoidance of pain – to another – one that is determined by the emergence of truth and desire for emotional growth. Therefore the causal notions that underpin much of Freud's theory and practice and which are present in a deep-rooted way in the minds of many analysts obstruct the mind from arriving at comprehension of the developmental process. In a similar way the pleasure principle, which is so germane to Freud's whole conceptualization, is antithetical to Bion's motivational principle, which is truth. The idea that someone would choose pain rather than evade it is quite foreign to Freud's way of thinking, especially as Bion conceives that such an event can occur very early in life.

Freud's notion of sexual libido is an obstruction to understanding Bion's descriptive analysis: an instance of the no-thing occupying a place where it should not be. Emotional growth has taken the place of sexual libido in Bion's formulation. Freud's notion of a symptom being the result of dammed-up libido finding an alternative channel of expression is deeply ingrained in analytic thinking. We believe, however, that it is contrary to analytic experience and the adherence to this belief blocks understanding of the analytic process. Some may think that in the more humanistic thinking of self-psychology Freud's assumptions have also been superseded. However, a closer inspection reveals that Hartmann's assumptions still underlie Kohut's formulations in that the governing force of the pleasure principle is still supreme.

As Bergson said, life tends we know not where. Bion's analysis attempts to be faithful to animate reality. Hence he says that use of the term 'mechanism' is inappropriate because it pertains to the inanimate not animate nature. The term 'mechanism', so frequently used by Kleinian analysts, is foreign to Bion's thinking and blocks understanding of Bion's analysis of the mind. We feel the need to emphasize this as it is clear to us that many Kleinians who use the term 'mechanism' and at the same time believe they are following Bion betray the fact that they are still conceptualizing within the paradigm of Kleinian theory and have failed to understand Bion.

Bion reversed Freud's dream theory. Whereas Freud thought that the dream's function was to conceal (yet reveal) a hidden wish, Bion thought its function was to synthesize fragmented elements into a whole.

Freud believed that the function of thought is for the reduction of tension, whereas Bion believed that it was for the management of tension. There is, then, a very fundamental difference between Freud and Bion in that the former's model posited a system whose function was the removal of pain and frustration whereas Bion posited a model where the individual was able to bear pain. Whereas Freud saw thought as a mode of achieving satisfaction for the organism, Bion saw thought as in the service of truth where the individual uses it to understand him- or herself. Freud's focus was on the external world which the human animal had to subdue in order to supply his or her survival needs, but Bion's was on the individual's self-conscious reflection. The individual's need for self-understanding has no place within Freud's conceptualization.

The most surprising Freudian concept which undergoes reformulation is the notion of the polarity conscious–unconscious. One of the most cherished beliefs is that psychoanalysis rests upon the unconscious and its relationship to consciousness, and yet Bion believes that this idea interferes with analytic understanding. Bion believes that the polarity conscious–unconscious needs to be replaced with finite–infinite. The infinite has no form, no categories, no number. He quotes Milton:

> The rising world of waters dark and deep
> Won from the void and formless infinite

> (Bion 1965: 151)

– to demonstrate the transforming process through which the infinite passes into finite grasp. We hope that in the process of this book the reader will grasp this polarity but we would ask the reader to free his mind of the notion of the unconscious and consciousness. If he does not it will certainly block his understanding of this process. Consciousness means awareness and this can be thought of as a different perspective upon events. This different perspective Bion called a 'vertex'. The different vertex supplants the theory of the unconscious and consciousness. There is another pitfall about using the term 'unconscious'. It is visualized as if the unconscious is a thing, so that people use phrases such as 'it was banished into the unconscious' as if the latter was a locality in the mind. We need to know instead why someone is not aware of something in himself. How this comes about is something to which Bion addresses himself.

In clinical practice there are frequent instances of this polarity finite–infinite. We will give two examples. A man came for analysis because his wife had suddenly said she was going to leave him. The analyst said to him:

> There seem to be two levels: one is a child pressing me to give you favours; to give you times that are more suitable to you, to see you at the weekend and to treat you with special consideration. The other is a clamour that pleads for no such favours because they bind you and lead you to feel 'obligated'; this clamour is for freedom from the pressures that are brought on your head by the spoilt child.

Now this remark had an import that related right through his life. As a child his parents had showered him with favours but then he had felt obligated towards them. In later life he had taken jobs that were not personally fulfilling, also out of obligation. This is also a 'life-problem' that has a relevance that most of us know; we might call it an eternal verity. It has the dimension that Bion called the infinite. Now the patient's immediate response to this interpretation was: 'Perhaps this is what I am doing wrong with Josephine. I must try and act differently towards her.' He has immediately circumscribed this. He has not taken it as an interpretation but as an instruction as to what he should *do*. He has changed its category from infinite to finite. The struggle in an analysis is to prevent the finite smothering the infinite.

Closely connected to his rejection of the conciousness–unconsciousness schema is his repudiation of the theory of primary and secondary processes. This is another foundation stone of the Freudian corpus. Bion referred instead to various levels of thinking, including the hypothetical concepts of beta elements and alpha elements. Alpha function is absent or deficient in the psychotic mind.

The last Freudian bastion that is implicitly demolished by Bion's approach is the structural model. The super-ego is replaced by the concept of a parasitic or mutually crushing interactive ♀ ♂ which depletes emotionality of its meaning;[2] the ego is finite – 'I must try to act differently towards Josephine' – and is replaced with evolution and the emergence of truth; and the id disappears as redundant. In one of the workshops Bion gave at the Tavistock in the late 1970s he said that he did not find the structural model useful.

---

[2] ♀ represents 'container' and ♂ represents 'contained'. See Chapter 6 below for further discussion.

BION AND THE KLEIN GROUP

The loyal disciples of Melanie Klein accept Bion's early work but are distrustful of his later work. One senior Kleinian said that Bion never wrote anything worthwhile after *Elements of Psycho-Analysis* (1963). Others believe that he deteriorated on leaving England and that everything he wrote subsequent to his departure is to be dismissed as the ramblings of a senile man. The cut-off point between that work which is acceptable to the Klein group and that which is not would seem to be either *Transformations* (1965) or *Attention and Interpretation* (1970). The question to which we now address ourselves is: why was the later Bion not acceptable to some Kleinians?

We believe the first reason was his introduction of 'O' which first appeared in *Transformations* and was further elaborated in *Attention and Interpretation*. Bion defines O thus:

> I shall use the sign O to denote that which is the ultimate reality represented by terms such as ultimate reality, absolute truth, the godhead, the infinite, the thing-in-itself.
>
> (Bion 1970: 26)

O, then, has a metaphysical and religious meaning. Melanie Klein was indifferent to religion and philosophy, though not opposed to them (Elliott Jaques, personal communication, 1995). Certain of her close followers, however, have, like Freud, been definitely anti-religious and almost fanatically opposed to any philosophical position which has any whiff of religion. They stand firmly in Freud's atheistic shoes and are pledged with him to positivism. When Bion introduced O, which is essentially a religious[3] and metaphysical concept, some in the Klein group were quick to dissociate themselves from his thinking from that time onwards.

A personal act of understanding is the goal of Bion's cognitive and emotional endeavour. Pre-conception seeking realization and the significance of the *selected fact* are both expressions of this intent. A personal act of understanding is, in its very nature, subversive or potentially subversive of received teaching. Some

---

[3]   By 'religious' we mean a model of the human being as a creature with intentionality that transcends immediate physical needs.

Kleinians have become the guardians of a new orthodoxy, which is a familiar phenomenon in the history of scientific movements. It has been poignantly described by Koestler:

> The new territory opened up by the impetuous advance of a few geniuses, acting as a spearhead, is subsequently occupied by the solid phalanxes of mediocrity; and soon the revolution turns into a new orthodoxy, with its unavoidable symptoms of one-sidedness, over-specialization, loss of contact with other provinces of knowledge, and ultimately, estrangement from reality. We see this happening – unavoidably, it seems – at various times in the history of various sciences. The emergent orthodoxy hardens into a 'closed system' of thought, unwilling or unable to assimilate new empirical data or to adjust itself to significant changes in other fields of knowledge.
>
> (Koestler 1975: 225)

Therefore Bion's prescription and encouragement towards a personal act of understanding stands as a threat to those anxious to maintain the purity of Melanie Klein's teaching. This attitude is always felt more strongly towards those who have been nurtured within a group's scientific culture. It has been said, for instance, that Salman Rushdie would not have incurred a *fatwa* if he had not been a Pakistani and a Muslim in upbringing. When the individual, by adopting a new personal perspective, separates from the group in which he or she was schooled, the group feels betrayed and closes ranks all the more rigidly.

It was only in his later works – say from *Attention and Interpretation* onwards – that the full implication of his earlier thinking became clear to the Kleinians.

Bion was closer to the Klein school than any other and many of his key concepts have been directly assimilated from Klein – projective identification, splitting, death instinct, paranoid-schizoid and depressive positions – but he used them in the service of a different outlook, a new metapsychology. He used the concept of death instinct in his papers on psychosis which have been gathered together in *Second Thoughts* (1967), but once he began to formulate his theory in *Learning from Experience* (1962), *Elements of Psycho-Analysis* (1963) and *Transformations* (1965) he no longer used it.

Kleinians are concerned with psychic reality, with inner objects, with psychic change, and so was Bion. Wherein lies the difference between Bion's approach and that of those who have remained faithful to Melanie Klein and Freud? There are several aspects which we could point to: for instance, Klein was more focused on the process of mental development and its disruption by forces like greed and envy. Bion's approach was more positive. His sphere of inquiry was more encompassing than what has been mentioned. He was concerned with our evolutionary past and where humankind is tending in the future. These are tendencies of mind, extremely important but not, we believe, the crux of the matter. Bion started from a reality which is unknown because unknowable, which he named O. This is quite foreign to the Kleinians and to Freud who preceded them. Their starting point is the raw mass of instinctual impulses. We have here two fundamentally different models of the individual and this differentiates Bion from Kleinians and Freudians. Starting from O or ultimate reality gave Bion a different perspective. Psychoanalysis became one expression of O; it was for Bion his point of entry into the sphere of O. One had a very definite impression listening to Bion that here was someone concerned with something wider and deeper than any one discipline and this was an attitude not shared by most of his colleagues either in the Klein group or in any of the other groups in the British Psycho-Analytical Society or those in America.

Bion went into analysis with Melanie Klein after the Second World War and apparently insisted to her that this was on condition that he was his own person when it came to thinking and reacting (Grosskurth 1985: 427). If this is true then we are witnessing the events of an independent thinker, influenced by Melanie Klein, but not a clone. The problem of the group in relation to such a person is a subject for another chapter.

The reader needs to purge her mind as far as possible of these 'tenets' of psychoanalytic faith. Adherence to these theories will block understanding of Bion's analysis of the analytic process. It is a shock to realize how iconoclastic Bion is with regard to Freud's theory. We believe, however, that if the reader tries to hold onto these Freudian tenets she will not understand the work of Bion. Bion uses some of Freud's theories and also some of Klein's theories and this leads analysts to believe that he was operating within their basic assumptions. This is incorrect. He used portions of their theory to explicate certain phenomena but his analytic description also implies a rejection of some basic tenets of the Freudian and Kleinian corpus.

Chapter 2

Bion: his character

*Whatever gifts of mind we have, henceforth to keep them under,
and to subject them to innocence, simplicity, and truth.*

(Newman 1876: 114)

If it is possible to isolate a central message which Bion bequeathed
to posterity it would be: *Think and speak from your own heart
and mind.* He addressed his mind to an analysis of experience.
Naturally this meant his own personal experience. In his autobiographical work *The Long Week-End* he tells how Asser, one
of his fellow officers, chose to be shot by the enemy rather than
surrender. His tank with all the crew inside was surrounded by
the enemy, who demanded the surrender of all those inside. Each
crew member came out with hands up and delivered himself over
to the enemy, but Asser came out last, gripping his Colt pistol,
showing the intention to fight, and he was instantly shot. Of this,
Bion wrote:

> I knew in my heart that if the enemy reached our trenches I
> could not go on fighting. I do not understand courage such as
> Asser's. I can easily understand all the *explanations* I have ever
> heard, but I cannot understand the thing itself.

(Bion 1982: 272)

Bion's mental effort was devoted to understanding *the thing itself.*
   The thing itself was so appalling that we think it likely that the
rest of his life was spent trying to assimilate it. At the tender age
of 19 he was summarily trained and rudely thrust to the front line
in command of a tank at Ypres. As he was standing talking to
Edwards, a fellow officer, he saw his brains blown out by an unexpected bullet. He saw Despard, an Irish tank commander, die by

his side. He was beside another officer who with his dying breath asked Bion to write to his mother. He found himself being persuaded by a German soldier to check whether his friend had died. Through the stupidity of an infantry commander he saw three of his tanks blow up in front of his eyes as they were clambering up a hill.

In the first three months of that war a million of the allied men had been killed. Bion was not the only one to pass through such an appalling trauma but we think he was probably one of the few who attempted to assimilate it and understand it. The mind can either dissociate from such an appalling experience or struggle to make sense of it – make sense not just of it but also of one's own responses to it – be they cowardly or courageous – which are not separable from it.

There is not a shadow of doubt that Bion was a man of outstanding courage. At the age of 19 he was faced with a crisis of appalling proportions – not just one crisis but an array of crises which, strung together, make a catastrophe. His courage was indisputable. He was recommended for the Victoria Cross but partly because of his own unwillingness he did not receive it but instead was awarded the Distinguished Service Order.

Bion insists upon his cowardice. We believe that this should be taken at face value as long as the reader remembers that an individual can only know his or her cowardice when it is not dominant in his or her personality. It is only the courageous individual who can know his or her cowardice.

CHILDHOOD

Bion was born in Muttra in the United provices of India in 1897 of English parents striving to remain in that exclusive club that comprises the English gentry. There are those who are born into it and with the wealth behind them to support it and make it possible, but there are also those who are in it but do not have that wealth and make extreme sacrifices to remain in it. Bion's parents were in the latter category. He was born into that class which George Orwell named 'the lower-upper-middle class' into which he himself was born. Orwell says the following of this class:

> I define it in terms of money, because that is always the quickest way of making yourself understood. Nevertheless, the essential

point about the English class-system is that it is *not* entirely explicable in terms of money. Roughly speaking it is a money-stratification, but it is also interpenetrated by a sort of shadowy caste-system; rather like a jerry-built modern bungalow haunted by medieval ghosts. Hence the fact that the upper-middle class extends or extended to incomes as low as £300 a year – to incomes, that is, much lower than those of merely middle-class people with no social pretensions. ...

To belong to this class when you were at the £400 a year level was a queer business, for it meant that your gentility was almost purely theoretical. You lived, so to speak, at two levels simultaneously. Theoretically you knew all about servants and how to tip them, although in practice you had one, at most, two resident servants. Theoretically you knew how to wear your clothes and how to order a dinner, although in practice you could never afford to go to a decent tailor or a decent restaurant. Theoretically you knew how to shoot and ride, although in practice you had no horses to ride and not an inch of ground to shoot over. It was this that explained the attraction of India (more recently Kenya, Nigeria, etc.) for the lower-upper-middle class. The people who went there as soldiers and officials did not go there to make money, for a soldier or an official does not want money; they went there because in India, with cheap horses, free shooting, and hordes of black servants, it was so easy to play at being a gentleman.

In the kind of shabby-genteel family that I am talking about there is far more *consciousness* of poverty than in any working-class family above the level of the dole. Rent and clothes and school-bills are an unending nightmare, and every luxury, even a glass of beer, is an unwarrantable extravagance.

(Orwell 1972: 106–8)

All his life Bion struggled to maintain himself and his family without capital, that unspoken upper-middle-class asset, while, at the same time, living among those who expected him and no doubt believed him to have wealth behind him. When he bought a house at Iver Heath after the Second World War he heard two gentlemen asking what sort of a fool could have £8,000 to throw away. Bion comments that he did not have £8,000 from lavish resources. So he had no capital but was thought to have it. We believe also that *one* of the reasons why he went to California in 1968 was to earn more money than he did in London and so accumulate some capital for his children.

There are certain trade marks of the English gentleman both instantly recognized by those in the club and envied by those outside it. The accent, the gestures of nonchalance, the disdain of the petty and a hundred other signs of membership that are not learned but imbibed in that expensive institution: the public school. The cost of sending a son to one of these schools is enormous and Bion's parents would have saved and scraped to make it possible for only by doing so could they hold their heads high. However, they could only manage by sending him to one of the lesser public schools. Bion tells his reader that in those *rites de passage* where he was seeking entry and acceptance into a new body he felt inferior. He had not been to Eton, Harrow or Winchester. He felt deeply humiliated when he was initially rejected by the army's recruiting office; he felt inferior when he first arrived at Oxford. By the time he was being interviewed by the Dean of Medicine at University College, London, in 1924 he managed to bring one of the necessary signs to force his acceptance: he had been in the First Fifteen at Oxford. He followed this up quickly with the information that he had captained the Oxford University swimming team and that did the trick. He had learned to use the trade marks to his advantage when it was necessary.

Public school starts at the age either of 14 or 12 and must be preceded by a sentence of four to six years in a 'prep school'. Thus it was that little Wilfred was sent off to school in England from distant India at the age of 8. So he underwent the 'full treatment' in the public school system. He gives the reader to understand that he had great difficulty in managing but that his competence at games saved the day for him. He suffered from the attitude of adults to children. He says that as a young child in India he had an experience well known to most Anglo-Saxon children. When he was relating something to grown-ups they would often laugh at him. This made him feel small and put him into a rage against them. This mocking laughter produced what psychoanalysts call a bad internal object. This was a frightening figure whom he named 'Arf Arfer'. The sense that he retreated into himself while surrounded by uncomprehending adults remained with him through his ten years of schooling, through his traumatic experiences in the army and through the remainder of his life. This retreat into himself was not an escape but what the French call *reculer pour mieux sauter*.

In horseplay at school one day he put a piece of string around another boy's neck and pulled it tight, whereupon the boy fell down unconscious. Bion loosened the string and the boy regained consciousness. He was worried by this so he asked a master impersonally as a matter of biological interest what the effects of such an action might be and he received an answer which did not reassure him. So he went the next day to the headmaster and made a clean breast of it. The headmaster told him that had there been a knot in the string so that he could not have loosened it the boy would have been dead in half a minute. The headmaster told him he was glad that Bion had come to him about it. The incident speaks for Bion's open-hearted honesty and also for a headmaster who respected it. The headmaster made an announcement the following day explaining the dangers of using string in horseplay without mentioning names. It could be that Bion's honesty and the headmaster's good sense saved the life of a luckless boy by prophylaxis.

THE FIRST WORLD WAR

Bion's experiences during the First World War were clearly so formative upon his psychological understanding of himself and human nature that we need to return to them in a bit more detail. He makes this arresting statement about himself: 'Many regard timidity as the disposition of a "milksop"' – flimsy, wayward, unreliable. In me it is the toughest, most robust, most enduring quality I have' (Bion 1982: 111–12). We think this connects with what we said about courage above. The courageous person feels fear whereas the reckless person does not. Paradoxically, then, timidity is the *sine qua non* of courage. The person who enjoys battle may not have the necessary foundation for courage. Bion says, 'I had not – then or since – known what it is to be seized by the joy of battle' (Bion 1982: 136).

It is interesting to contrast this attitude with that of Winston Churchill, who was in command of the 6th Royal Scots Fusiliers in 1916 at the same time as Bion was at the Front. Captain Gibb wrote this of Churchill, 'I profoundly hated war. But at that and every moment I believe Winston Churchill revelled in it. There was no such thing as fear in him . . .' (quoted in Bonham Carter

1965: 44). With Churchill there was no consciousness of fear. Churchill was also totally identified with the British Empire and its causes. Bion was conscious of fear, conscious of his own inner states; he was also not identified with Britain and its patriotic purposes. He was always conscious of himself as separate from the group, analysing its nature and questioning its purposes. He was one of the most extreme examples of the outsider. We define the outsider as one who is not identified with the several groups of which he is a member. Churchill was excited by the sound of bullets whistling as they whizzed close by. We believe that what incorporates the individual into the group so that he or she is a cohesive, unaware part of it is precisely this 'excitement', which is the subjective experience of the process of projective identification. Bion's connection to the group was through thought; Churchill's was through erotic ecstasy. That Bion dissociates himself from what we might call the Churchill attitude can be seen from the following passage:

> One day, years after the war, I was swimming at a popular road house and was accosted by another swimmer. He had recognized me, but it took me a moment or two before there emerged from out of the matrix of the firm businessman's face the pink baby-face of Broome.
>
> 'Those days of the war – when I look back at them,' he said, 'were the happiest days of my life.'
>
> 'Impossible,' I replied.
>
> 'They were. I enjoyed every moment of it.'
>
> Every moment; fancy that. I really believe that prosperous businessman was speaking the truth.
>
> (Bion 1982: 140)

It is clear that Bion was amazed and it was the sort of phenomenon he studied with earnest intent in his years as a psychoanalyst.

Bion was preoccupied to know what lay behind external appearances. He says of the Colonel of his regiment, 'He was as usual immaculate. Sometimes such dress is an expression of the personality; sometimes a substitute for a personality that is not there. There are times when it is imperative to know which is which' (Bion 1982: 150). Despard, the comrade mentioned above, was killed by a bullet in the belly. Before he died he said: '"I knew it. When that bloody . . . magpie . . . came this morning," he gasped, "I knew my number was up"' (Bion 1982: 135). Bion goes on to say: 'I felt stunned. I could not think what to say to this queer fatalistic Irishman. How could he possibly be convinced, as he was, that a magpie was more obviously the cause of death than a bullet' (Bion 1982: 135). In later years Bion was to trace the origins of superstitions such as this.

Bion led his tank crew in the offensive at Cambrai in France. He describes vividly how he drove the tank through a barricade of barbed wire which was 6 feet high and 10 feet deep. Once he had penetrated through these defences he drove the tank 'blind' (the hatches being closed against enemy fire) towards the enemy position. The compass that gave him a bearing on the direction in which he should steer was that part of the tank being most heavily peppered with bullets. He was unaware of having been hit. It took his second in command to point out that he was pouring blood. He refers to it though as just a 'flesh wound'. Soon after, the tank came to a full-stop and was in danger of catching fire with its 90 gallons of petrol and masses of ammunition. Bion and his crew jumped out and took possession of an enemy trench. Here they were fired upon from above, whereupon Bion leaped out and returned fire at their assailants, prompting the swift retreat of a detachment of German soldiers.

For his bravery Bion was, as we have seen, recommended for the Victoria Cross. He did not believe he deserved this as he thought his crew's merit was equal to his own. When he was interviewed by the General he was asked whether he wanted the honour and he said, 'Oh yes, Sir, very much ... well, not really, Sir' (Bion 1982: 173). Carter, a fellow officer, asked him afterwards how the interview had gone and whether he got the VC. Bion replied:

> 'I shouldn't think so – I couldn't think of anything to say' and Carter replied,
> 'You ought to have learned up your part beforehand.'
> (Bion 1982: 173–4)

Bion said he could not understand what lay in the mind of this disillusioned man. It is clear that Bion did not lust after position, status or the outer signs of these. It also seems he did not understand the minds of those for whom this motivation is all-consuming. He understood the burden that honours can put upon a person. Many years later, after having been President of the

British Psycho-Analytical Society, he left for California. One motive was to escape the burden of honours to give himself the time to develop his mind and to think and to write. He says a bit further on:

> I could understand why a VC was virtually a sentence of death; why men said that winners of the VC either broke down and found a soft job in England, or were killed subsequently trying to deserve the honour they had won.
>
> (Bion 1982: 190)

To make sense of this one has to appreciate that Bion says that he was in some kind of anaesthetized state when he did the actions for which he was decorated with the Distinguished Service Order. His assumption is that this is also so of others: that they are unconscious of their bravery and when they are decorated for it they wrestle to cope with it – either repudiating it or desperately trying to live up to it.

In *The Long Week-End* there are 183 pages devoted to the war. They are full of pain, tragedy and waste. It seemed only a matter of time before Bion would be killed, and yet when on leave visiting his mother down in Cheltenham he says, 'Relations with anyone I respected were intolerable, notably with my mother; I wanted nothing except to get back to the Front just to get away from England and from her' (Bion 1982: 266). The appalling carnage of the war was preferable to being with his mother. It is said that Richard III had a frightening dream the night before the battle of Bosworth Field which made him say to Ratcliffe:

> By the apostle Paul, shadows tonight
> Have struck more terror to the soul of Richard
> Than can the substance of ten thousand soldiers
> Armed in proof and led by shallow Richmond.
>
> (*King Richard III*, Act V, Scene III, vv. 216–20)

Being with mother, not shadows, struck more terror into the soul of Wilfred than the substance of a hundred thousand soldiers being slaughtered at the Front. His mother may have been objectively terrible but this is not the sense that he conveys about her because he says she was someone he respected; rather, he had invested her with some monstrous shadows from within. On a previous occasion when he came back from the Front to receive the Distinguished Service Order from the King at Buckingham Palace he says:

> My mother, defeated and helpless in the face of my taciturn moroseness, asked if I knew the riddle of the miser's most hated flower. 'It's the anemone,' she said, 'because it reminds him of someone saying "Any money? Any money?"' My response was a stony silence which was so hostile that it frightened me.
>
> (Bion 1982: 190)

This gives a picture of a woman trying to humour her sullen son, perhaps with a levity that was insensitive to his mood, but nevertheless with kind intent. His hatred of her resulted from a projection that turned her into a dark presence, the intensity of which frightened him. Even at this stage, then, he was aware that his worst enemy, the one that frightened him most, was within. This one was worse than all, even than all the horrors of war. Herein lies the embryonic analyst. We may conjecture that it was through a knowledge of his own soul that he came to understand so well the psychotic in the personality. It was also the seed of his later mysticism.

BION'S CHARACTER

Values are integral to character. A person for whom power and position are the dominating foci of the personality is a very different character to someone, like Bion, who values truth and the achievement of love above all else. It is these focal values which differentiate character structure – the man of honour from the charlatan, the deceitful woman from the faithful woman and so on. It is important to separate the theories of an analyst from his own person, but we also believe that some insights are only possible to the one in whom the values of truth and love are central. If the mind is healed by truth, then how can a psychoanalyst primarily motivated by desire for prestige, say, manage to relay truth to his patients? We distrust therefore the theories of someone whose focal values do not correspond to a desire to achieve love, freedom and pursuit of truth. It is difficult to assess a person's values because they are inner and are usually not known consciously by many. Bion's widow, Francesca, has, we believe, done a service to the psychoanalytic world by publishing his love letters to her during the time of their courtship and at times in their marriage when they were apart. In no sphere are someone's focal values more visible than in such intimate communications. There is no substitute for reading those letters, which have been published in *All My Sins Remembered* and *The Other Side of Genius* (1985). Here we will make the briefest précis of his character as it emerges in these letters.

What emerges most clearly is the simplicity of the man. In our sophisticated world this quality may be derided, but wise men and women have seen it differently. One such wise man was Fenelon, who was Archbishop of Cambrai in the seventeenth century:

> In the world, when people call anyone simple, they generally mean a foolish, ignorant, credulous person. But real simplicity, so far from being foolish, is almost sublime. All good men like and admire it, are conscious of sinning against it, observe it in others and know what it involves; and yet they could not precisely define it. I should say that simplicity is an uprightness of soul which prevents self-consciousness. It is not the same as sincerity, which is a much humbler virtue. Many people are sincere who are not simple. They say nothing but they believe to be true, and do not aim at appearing anything but what they are. But they are for ever thinking about themselves, weighing their every word and thought, and dwelling upon themselves in apprehension of having done too much or too little. These people are sincere but they are not simple. . . . Real simplicity lies in a *juste milieu* equally free from thoughtlessness and affectation, in which the soul is not overwhelmed by externals, so as to be unable to reflect, nor yet given up to the endless refinements which self-consciousness induces. That soul which looks where it is going without losing time arguing over every step, or looking back perpetually, possesses true simplicity. Such simplicity is indeed a great treasure. How shall we attain to it ? I would give all I possess for it.
>
> (quoted in Huxley 1980: 130–1)

Just as it is difficult to define simplicity so also it is difficult to marshal evidence for its presence in Bion, and yet in his letters to Francesca and to his children it shines through. Just one quote from a letter to Francesca and one to one of the children must suffice:

> If this is a dream it is the longest and most marvellous dream I have ever had; if it is not a dream, then I don't know how

to contain myself. My goodness, I think, how lovely, how lovely she is. And she has promised to marry *me*. How extraordinary! I must have got myself muddled up with someone else. Whatever shall I do? Will she be very disappointed when she finds out what a dreadfully ordinary person I am? And then I feel rather sad. And then I begin to hope that you like rather ordinary people and that you really know I am ordinary and love me just the same. Is that right ? *Do* say it's right. My dearest Francesca, if only I could tell you how I feel. How excited and how nervous.

(Bion 1985: 95)

In my room in Harley Street there is a small window. I keep it open so as to have plently of fresh air. But now a pigeon has built its nest just above where it opens. And the pigeon has some eggs and is hatching a brood of young ones. I don't know how the mother bird is going to find food for them when they come. I hope they will not make too much noise. My patients won't like it if they do.

(Bion 1985: 170)

There are some beautiful letters to the children which have been printed in his own handwriting with little drawings he made to illustrate things he describes. Understood correctly we would say that simplicity was the dominant feature of his character. He acknowledges in one of his letters that he was able to see with clarity the important issues in a problematic situation. Such a capacity to go to the heart of the matter is one of the attributes of simplicity. We believe that this was the central organizing principle of his personality.

An analyst in London, Maureen Brook, now dead, used to look with wonder at a filing cabinet in Bion's consulting-room when going to him for supervision. She imagined it stacked with learned papers. One day, however, at the end of the supervision he offered her a cup of tea, which she accepted; then, out of the top drawer of the filing cabinet came a tea-pot and out of the next came milk, sugar and tea! Albert Mason took to him for supervision a very disturbed patient who used to get up in the night and switch on the light to see if he was still in bed or not. Bion listened to this, stroked his moustache with a twinkle in his eye and said, 'Well, we're all entitled to a second opinion.' We wish to try to capture what he valued most in life – what a sociologist would term his 'values'. For him happiness and contentment arose from loving his wife and family and being loved by them. He expresses this clearly in a letter to Francesca during their courtship:

> Your love is the most precious thing in the world to me and when I have that, you need not think I need more. I am a very ordinary sort of man my dearest, but with your love I shall also be a happy one and no one can ask for more than that. Success, as the world rates it, and outward show are quite agreeable if they come along but they are very much by products which I think come a very long way behind ordinary contentment and happiness.
>
> (Bion 1985: 91)

This was the most precious thing to him and therefore it followed that he put extreme value upon the effort to maintain it and enhance it:

> I so deeply feel that we can build a really happy life and home that it almost makes me afraid. One has seen so many people who seem to have everything with which to build up something really worth while – and then they have just frittered it all away till all that is left is a monument to ineptitude and pettiness. The most ghastly fate, made all the more tragic because it is so unspectacular; just a failure here and another little failure there, multiplied a few hundred times and the trick is done. Well, we must hope to do better; you will have to help me play my part better than I have managed so far.
>
> (Bion 1985: 97)

That type of worldly cynicism that shrugs its shoulders at yet another shattered relationship was entirely foreign to him. The bonds between himself and his loved ones mattered. Doing things properly and in a worthwhile manner was what he put effort into. To one of his children he wrote:

> It is terrible to skim over a job and get a superficial smattering that is nothing more than a facile covering up for ignorance. It is an easy but awful habit to get into because you then go on bluffing even if there is no need to do so. Don't make the mistake of thinking any worthwhile job that is done properly will ever feel easy. Unfortunately, fooling one's self and others is both easy and *not* worthwhile.
>
> (Bion 1985: 174)

It was clear what he valued. There were objects which were worthwhile. By 'objects' we mean those human beings to whom he had bound himself and those human realities which he served. Of these realities psychoanalysis would be one, others would be truth and beauty. When engaged in work for either category of these objects it was worth putting all his energy into making the best job possible. Shot through with simplicity his person became luminous to those who loved him. When he died this was summed up in the words of his 7-year-old grand-daughter: 'I didn't realize I knew Grandpa so well' (Bion 1985: 243).

A psychoanalyst's task is to come to know his patients. He can achieve this through self-knowledge. Bion had espoused this goal and achieved it. We believe that he achieved an understanding of the mind that has not been surpassed by any other analyst.

Chapter 3

The emotional catalyst

What does have a lasting effect? Anything that stimulates, mobilizes, creates feelings belonging to the love–hate spectrum.

(Bion 1991: 362)

Bion's concern is the application of thought to emotional experience. The question then arises: 'What is it that triggers emotional experience?' And his answer is: 'An emotional experience cannot be conceived of in isolation from a relationship' (Bion 1962b: 42). The ecological niche that gives birth to emotional experience is the relationship of one human being with another. Bion reduces the links between human beings to Love (L), Hate (H) and Knowledge (K) and the negatives of each of these which he abbreviated to –L, –H and –K. At first sight it may appear too schematic to reduce the emotional current flowing between people to these six, and yet, under psychoanalytic investigation, the rationale for this reduction becomes plausible. Let us say that I fear someone – into which of these six categories will it be placed? It could be categorized under L, H, –L or –H. If I love someone I may fear his or her rejection; if I hate someone I may fear his or her retaliation; if I block loving feelings I may fear being cold-shouldered, and similarly if I block hate I may fear withdrawal. Emotional activities that are blocked are still active and therefore the individual still fears a reaction. Fear is what I experience as a would-be receiver. It needs to be noted that Bion's six links are all emotional *activities*.[1] Fear is a *passivity*. The passivities are all consequent upon the *activities* so the latter are primary. But we can also think

---

[1] 'Like L and H, K represents an active link and has about it a suggestion that if *x* K *y* then *x* does something to *y*' (Bion 1962b: 47).

of emotional activities which are not included in Bion's six links, such as trust, for example. However Bion's categories are like general files into which go other linking emotions; so, for instance, trust goes under L and greed goes under H. We are making the point that all emotions can therefore be conceptualized under these six links.

The K link is that linkage present when one is in the process of getting to know the other in an emotional sense, and this is to be clearly distinguished from the sort of knowing that means having a piece of knowledge about someone or something. A somewhat similar distinction is made in languages such as Italian, French, Spanish, Portuguese and German, in which a different verb is used when referring to knowing the facts from that used for getting to know what someone is like.

This distinction can easily be seen in relationships in the outside world as well as in the analytic session. A patient may try to extract facts from the analyst or theories to explain his symptoms, rather than risking an emotional engagement with the analyst. The process of getting to know involves pain, frustration and lone-liness. Obtaining a piece of knowledge about a person does not involve these states, in fact it is like cannibalism, taking some-thing and avoiding emotional involvement.

> He bashes in [the woman's] skull. God! It's like rock. He treats it like eggshell. He's sucking – this is cannibalism! He sucks out the brain. . . . The darkness deepens. The skull-crushing and sucking object is overwhelmed by depression at the failing supply of nutriment from the dead ♀ and the failure to restore it to life.
>
> (Bion 1991: 159, 161)

In an analytic session, the couple may achieve an understanding through the K relationship only to find that it then degenerates into having a piece of intellectualized knowledge of it. This reversal occurs as a way of evading the painful realization achieved through the K link. In a similar way, having a piece of knowledge about oneself is not at all the same as getting to know oneself through experiencing those aspects of the self in the rela-tionship with the analyst. To come upon one's ruthless greed in relation to another is quite a different matter from intellectual awareness of it. There is a continuing decision to be made as to whether to evade pain or to tolerate and thus modify it. The reversal referred to above is an evasion of pain.

The link is a crucial activity in which the emotional experience of learning takes place. Hatred of learning, deriving from the psychotic part of the personality, leads to an attack on the link, resulting in the process being stopped and even reversed. Thus, instead of meaning developing, or thinking being promoted, there occurs a reversal of the process so that any meaningful units become stripped of their meaning.

Forces against the emotional experience being understood are legion, both within the individual and within society. These forces, as expressed within the relationship, are represented as the negative of the L, H and K links; thus –L, –H and –K. If one of these negative links is dominating, the process of understanding within the relationship is stopped and reversed; meaningful experience may be destroyed.

Although looking at a number of consecutive associations in an analytic session might give the idea that every association represents a different emotional link, now H, now K and so on, in practice it is possible to define the key emotional link of each analytic session, that which underlies all the other statements and feelings; rather like the key signature at the commencement of a piece of music. In this way, all other remarks in the session, including the analyst's interpretations, can be looked at with reference to this key signature. It does not define the transference nor yet is it a record of emotional experiences in the session, but it should be the case that all the parts of the session do relate to this key link. It is like a standard against which other statements can be measured. Defining the key emotional link of the session in this way contributes to understanding at a deeper level and prevents wild analytic theorizing by providing a base for the analyst's imagination. Bion describes this key link as a working tool for use in the session. A value is put on this key link and all other statements receive their relative value from that. Value therefore resides in these key links.

For example: a young boy comes into his session in an unruly way. He crashes some cars together, makes menacing feints at the therapist, but settles when his anger and time-wasting have been discussed. He then talks lucidly about his refusal to join in some sexual game at school. The lucid talk is interrupted by further messing up, throwing the Playdough around, spilling water on the floor and spitting. These are the sexual games in which he is now again a participant, having briefly resisted them for a time while he was talking to the therapist. The key note of this session could be H. He is someone capable of arousing hatred of himself in others by his provocative behaviour. He has demonstrated smashing attacks between the cars, swipes at the therapist, messing with Playdough and water. The therapist thinks, however, that the key is to be found in an attitude that is against the emergence of tender feelings. Any impulse towards the loving side is wiped out as soon as it threatens to emerge. The key here seems to be not so much H as a reversal of love, hence –L. Further into the session, he blocks out the therapist's voice as she tries to make an interpretation, and what he does hear, he mocks. This might also suggest a hatred of the emotional experience involved in getting to know himself: –K, but –L was chosen because there was clear evidence of a periodic breaking through of the wish to co-operate which was almost instantaneously overridden by another attack on the toys or the room.

So the catalyst which gives rise to the emotional experience is the link between one human being and another. It is out of this emotional experience that either a thought process or a discharge will take place. (We examine this process in the next chapter on the Grid.) Without the links there would be no emotional experience and without that no development of thought. It is therefore the foundation stone without which there would be no edifice.

Chapter 4

The Grid

It is a well-founded historical generalization, that the last thing to be discovered in any science is what the science is really about.
(Whitehead 1958: 167)

Bion had worked on the thinking processes in groups and in psychotic patients. He then applied his mind to the conceptualization of the thinking process in general. The Grid describes the essence of his elucidation of the growth of thought.

This chapter explains Bion's concept of the Grid. As the book proceeds, the reader will be referred back to the Grid. We do not expect that the reader will have understood the Grid when he or she has finished reading this chapter. We are laying out the Grid as a ground plan, like a chess-board onto which the chess pieces can be placed as the reader travels through the book.

The psychoanalytic investigation takes place in the relationship between analyst and patient. The increasing comprehension of what constitutes the psychoanalytic process and Bion's attempts to deepen this understanding can be likened to the development of an understanding of the evolution of the concept of numbers.

It must have required many ages to discover that a brace of pheasants and a couple of days were both instances of the number 2: the degree of abstraction involved is far from easy.
(Russell 1993: 3)

Many ages might be required also to distil out the essence of the psychoanalytic process.

The evolution of numeracy in early civilizations began with merely the idea of 'a lot' or 'a few', that is, an idea of a pile of objects being larger or smaller. Next there developed the idea of a number of objects, the number indicating the amount of the substance. This number was felt to be the property of the collection of objects. This was reflected in vocabulary in that in certain languages there were no separate words for numbers, rather the words for numbers denoted them as numbers of some particular object. Thus five, for example, was the number of fingers on a hand; it was a property of the hand, but there was no word for the number five on its own. In the neolithic period, clay tokens were used to record transactions of grain, oil and sheep (Schmandt-Besserat 1992). The requisite number of tokens was placed in a clay envelope which was subsequently sealed. Before doing so each separate token was impressed on the outside of the clay envelope to indicate how many were inside, thus creating a one-to-one correspondence between marks and tokens. It was only realized much later that a sign on the outside of the envelope was enough to record the amount without having to place the tokens inside. This step, which to us sounds so trivial, would have occurred in a supreme moment of insight. Finally number was recognized as an abstract idea.

The progressive clarification of what the analytic process consists of is still taking place. By means of abstraction we try to find more general principles that underlie our present practice. Breuer recognized the importance of reclaiming the repressed elements in the mind from the unconscious. He thus made a start in reclaiming some sort of order from chaos, like distinguishing 'a lot' from 'a few'. Freud then understood that this reclamation took place in the setting and through interpretation of the transference relationship. Klein greatly elaborated the significance of internal objects and in so doing described the inner world of object relations. This evolution resembles the development in early civilizations from perceiving merely 'a lot' to understanding a one-to-one correspondence between tokens and produce. Bion took a greater step in abstraction when he recognized that underlying all this was what he termed the psychoanalytic object, O, representations of which could be descried in the session, by meaning evolving out of a relationship. We have moved with Bion perhaps to the point where neolithic humans realized that the clay envelope with the impressions on its outside meant that it was not necessary to have tokens inside. Bion believed that we are still at a primitive level of development.

What is being described here is the process of mental growth from a primitive delineation which is a first attempt to wrest something from chaos, to a highly sophisticated and abstract idea. The Grid is an attempt to describe the progressive development of thought from concrete to highly abstract levels. It represents the means by which the undifferentiated becomes differentiated or how the form or idea becomes distilled out of what is incarnate; that is, how the truth is made manifest.

Put in another way, we have seen how, over a great space of time, the concept of number, a very complex idea, gradually became clarified. Each analytic session gives us a chance to delineate the process of psychoanalysis. Out of the conversation taking place in the session, admittedly not an ordinary conversation, aspects of the truth, of the reality between the patient and the analyst, are gradually delineated. This 'conversation', although it consists of words and also of silences, is, for analytic purposes, the formless matrix from which islands of clarity are won.

If we think about how understanding dawns in a session, we realize that a certain process has occurred leading up to this, a certain momentum has developed. The Grid concerns this process of the session, in particular the form of the statements made by both analyst and patient and the use to which they are put in the session. By attempting to classify statements in this way, a new understanding into the evolving nature of the psychoanalytic process develops.

The Grid, then, is an attempt to represent elements of thought in the process of development and in their use. The function of psychoanalysis is to elucidate this development. Bion said that psychoanalysis was not a perfect instrument to achieve this purpose but that he did not know a better one.

THE GRID

The Grid displays certain features of the analytic session in such a way as to reveal their dynamic qualities and interrelatedness. It is comprised of two axes and the points plotted on these two axes derive from the nature of the statements made in the session, either the analyst's interpretations or the patient's associations or both. It is an attempt to explain our thinking activities by focusing on what is happening in the analytic session. It is a practical tool for increasing the analyst's awareness and understanding of what both he and the patient are doing. It is for use in review rather than during the actual session. It also enables comparison to be made between the nature of the patient's response and the nature of an interpretation.

Each of the Grid's two axes gives a perspective on the development of thought. We shall deal first with the horizontal axis, which comprises the use to which thoughts can be put.

The horizontal axis – the use to which thoughts may be put

Bion realized that statements made by both analyst and patient can have many different uses. This was a simple insight but extremely useful. The Grid provides a structure in which these varying uses can be examined and clarified.

The psychoanalytic process can be seen as one in which different viewpoints of the patient's personality are being elucidated by an understanding of what happens in the current relationship with the analyst. Interpretation facilitates the process of exploration and progressively approximates to the O of the session, that is, the psychoanalytic object, realization of which is the aim of psychoanalysis. Everything that happens in the session is generated by the emotional activity existing between analyst and patient. This is an instance of one of the links (L, H, K, –L, –H or –K) generating an emotional field.

The analytic endeavour is to build up understanding to the point at which an interpretation will emotionally move the patient, thus revealing the path to change. This may be achieved in stages. The various ways in which interpretations can be used are graded according to their power to elicit covert material and therefore to initiate change; in other words, they can be graded in terms of increasing confrontation of the patient by what he shuns knowing, his denied self. The Grid defines these steps, so that it should be possible, when the Grid has been understood, to look back over a session and classify the various statements of patient and analyst in the ways outlined below.

On commencing to investigate any subject, first approximations are made to define it. This first tentative definition or hypothesis creates a loose boundary around the subject, and, from this, further approximations may delineate it more clearly. In the example of the development of the concept of number, the initial stage was of naming a pile of objects, either 'a lot' or 'a few'.

Analyst and patient meet in a situation of more or less hidden chaos. To begin to understand something in this chaos attempts might be made to put a name to an idea or a feeling state of the patient. For example, an analyst might say, 'I think you are feeling depressed', with the meaning that what the patient is describing is what the analyst would label 'depression'. The remark is a definition and an hypothesis. It is a starting point of the investigation. It aims to define the situation and to give it a boundary. The statement means merely the opinion of this particular analyst. It cannot be right or wrong, but by communicating an idea to the patient the exploration into the chaotic or unbounded state of affairs has begun. These *definitory hypotheses* form column 1 of the Grid. Such an hypothesis defines both what is within the boundary of the definition and therefore also what is without and thereby excluded from the definition.

The next stage is *notation*, column 3, where facts are gathered together. This is like the function of memory – it provides storage of material from where it can be retrieved when wanted. A description of events might fall into this category. Also those occasions in analysis when the patient and analyst take note of some significant fact from the current or previous session. This marks something as significant, with the connotation of beginning to get to know something, the first step in confrontation. It could also represent a progression from the definitory hypothesis.

For instance, following an interpretation which has made sense to the patient, there may be a short period of co-operative work followed by a change to something that opposes communication. The material may seem, for example, to be intellectualized, boring, haranguing or repetitive. The analyst in effect asks the patient to take note of this occurrence as a first step in exploring its significance. As another example we take the occasion when the patient has used a particular image or unusual word on more than one occasion in the same session. The analyst may want the patient to note this so that this interesting fact does not get lost.

The notation interpretation is to be distinguished from the sort of comment which derives from the analyst's anxiety to show that he understands, when in fact he does not. In this case he may find himself searching in his mind for previously understood material to try to make sense of the current situation, and, from this, may refer back to a previous session, away from the more difficult and incomprehensible material of the current session: such a procedure by the analyst would be a column 2 intervention. This is discussed more fully later in this chapter.

As the process of understanding escalates, the analyst draws the patient's attention to the analyst's hypothesis about the current material. It is a statement which is more probing than the previous category and has a sense of searching for something that will complete or confirm it. Such *attention* interpretations are classified in column 4 of the Grid. It is a state of mind which is able to discriminate between similar presentations of differing significance. It is from this state of mind that there is receptiveness to the 'selected fact', that which suddenly illuminates the meaning of several previously observed facts. This selected fact is discussed Chapter 10.

This occurs, for example, when a patient responds to an interpretation by saying 'I don't agree with you'. This could be a straightforward expression of wishing to have nothing to do with any interpretation, but it could be an expression of looking closely at the interpretation for the purpose of getting closer to the truth. The analyst's state of mind will be attentive to that difference and a column 4 interpretation would draw the patient's attention to this difference, namely, that the patient's attitude is different and shows an interest in the analytic inquiry.

Next are those interpretations whose aim is to seek to obtain further information by probing more actively the particular area under focus and to elicit from the patient more active attempts to explore the depths of his own personality which he might not otherwise do. These are referred to as interpretations of *inquiry*, column 5. These interpretations of increasingly active investigation arise out of analytic work that keeps focused on the point of maximum anxiety for the analyst, rather as Bion aimed his 'blinded' tank in the direction from which the bullets were coming at their thickest. It may be a probing towards eliciting unowned feelings or thoughts.

Finally in this list of interpretations of increasing challenge are those which confront the patient with an irrefutable fact about himself that, if heeded and thought about, can lead to psychic change. These are *action* interpretations of column 6 and may be preceded by a sense of anxiety in the analyst, who is aware of the reaction that might be precipitated in the patient by this challenge to his defences, the shock of suddenly feeling vulnerable, separate or wounded. At this moment the analyst is faced with a sense of his own isolation.

Although this is a slight diversion it is worth noting at this point that the patient may bypass these 'action' interpretations. He is faced with the choice of whether to use the interpretation to further his own development or to waste it by ignoring it, or using it in an external situation. We gave the example in Chapter 1 of the man who converted an interpretation from the infinite realm to the finite. Another example: a patient who is himself a therapist may use the interpretation in the therapy of one of his own patients. Another patient may be uncertain as to whether or not to give up a frustrating relationship with her boyfriend. She may use the analyst's interpretation as advice about this external problem, thus delaying the development of her own capacity to make these decisions. So, although the interpretation has the potential to elicit change, the patient's response may block this. The following example illustrates this point and it will be used again to demonstrate the Grid categories.

A young man claimed that once again he had given up drugs. He gave a plausible story over the next three days as to his understanding of the internal propaganda to which he expected to be exposed in this struggle. In one session, after giving the analyst a rather overbearing lecture about the corrupt nature of the government and people in general, he said that he had been keeping something from the analyst, namely, that he had not yet given up the drugs. Next, with a mixture of curiosity and embarrassment he commented that he had experienced a sexual feeling as he told this news. The analyst reminded him of the many occasions when he had built up the hopes of someone close to him, only to destroy and mess up whatever had been achieved, and that he was now attempting to do this with the analyst. It could then be seen that in this pursuit of sadistic sexual excitement he was sacrificing his own development. Briefly he was shocked to see this but then he said quickly that although he could see that he was doing it, he could immediately distance himself from it as though it were another person perpetrating it. Here the choice to develop was present but was followed by immediate evasion.

Column 2, designated by the Greek letter psi (ψ), remains to be described. Interpretations falling in this column are those made by the analyst in order to reassure himself that he understands what is going on but in fact he does not. It is made when the analyst cannot tolerate not understanding the material and therefore of having to wait for clarification of the analytic situation to occur. It is a case of the analyst not being able to bear frustration. He tells himself that he knows and makes an interpretation accordingly. By making this untruthful statement the unfolding of the real meaning of the current situation is interrupted. Thus column 2 interpretations prevent the emergence of something else which could reveal the truth. This sort of interpretation is an attempt to bypass the pain associated with not understanding, and with uncertainty. An analyst might make this sort of statement when he feels under pressure from the patient to say something but is not convinced that what he has to say is either true or contributes to the patient's understanding. In other words, these interpretations are against the analytic inquiry. Statements in this column are evidence that a –K link is in operation.

We are currently looking at the Grid mainly from the point of view of the analyst's interpretations, but the patient's associations can also be classified according to the use to which they are being put. Some other examples of classification can be taken from the patient's material immediately above, even though it is not all from one session.

The young man's claim that he had given up drugs could be seen as belonging to column 3 if it is a fact to be taken into account, column 4 if a warning to the analyst, or even column 6 if its intention was to provoke the analyst. It could fall into column 2 if it was used to prevent the emergence of truth. His talk about the internal propaganda to which he would now be subjected indicated his wish to show the analyst that he knew what would happen and therefore had no need of the analyst. It was a churning out of stale material to have an effect on the analyst and would therefore be categorized as an action, column 6. The overbearing lecture in its unthinking tone aroused suspicion in the analyst and was thought of as a column 2 statement. It could also be seen as a discharging of dead material, column 6. His next two statements about wanting to inform the analyst that he had been withholding information and was actually still on drugs showed that he was thinking about his real situation, and they were in the service of the analytic inquiry and drew attention to a dangerous situation, column 4. Reporting the awareness of sexual feelings can be seen as further pursuit of self-knowledge, column 5. The analyst's interpretation, while including a column 4 element, was basically a column 6 statement intended to move the patient emotionally. Having felt shocked by this, the patient again drew the analyst's attention to his immediate moving away from contact. This was column 4 briefly and then column 6 as he moved into action and mentally disengaged, in which process he got rid of the shock of something emotionally meaningful. This is an example of the link changing from K to –K.

These differing uses of interpretation comprise the horizontal axis of the Grid, with increasing confrontative or probing power related to the movement across the columns from left to right. Thus columns 1, 3, 4, 5 and 6 hold the use categories *definitory hypothesis*, *notation*, *attention*, *inquiry* and *action* with the meanings as outlined above. It is important to note that each of these interpretations or associations could be worded in exactly the same way but yet have different uses.

The vertical axis – the genetic development of thoughts

The vertical axis comprises the various stages in the development of thoughts from their primitive matrix through to their most abstract form. This will be dealt with in detail in later chapters but for the present certain terms with which the reader will become familiar need to be explained. The primitive matrix from which thoughts develop, the unprocessed and unthought data, are named beta elements. These are categorized in the first horizontal line of the Grid, row A. Immediately following this in row B are alpha elements, which are the primitive elements of thought derived from the basic data of the mind by the process of alpha function, although it needs to be understood that both beta and alpha elements and alpha function are hypothetical entities. The subsequent rows contain elements which definitely exist.

Row C is basically a descriptive category and comprises *dream thoughts*, *dreams* and *myths*, that is, anything that is expressible in terms of sensuous images, commonly visual. This includes narrative. For example, a description of daily events conjures up a visual image. The term 'myth' requires further explication as it includes not only typical social myths such as that of Oedipus, but also a person's representation of an event. This is a myth in the sense that any one person's description of an event is his or her own unique view of it. No event can be described without this personal element nor can it be accurately recorded, even using mechanical aids such as a tape-recording or a photographic record, because these also leave out many qualities. Thus the patient's description of an event or an analyst's description of a session are each a personal myth of what happened and would be categorized in row C.

Although dreams are usually experienced visually, they may make themselves felt in modes other than the visual. In his later writings, Bion even suggests that bodily symptoms may be an expression of a dream.

Row D is the category of the *pre-conception*. This is a very important category to understand because it is the basic mechanism in the process of which mental growth occurs. The pre-conception is open to, and searching for, a particular experience with which it can match up and then be complete. This mating renders it emotionally real and is associated with the subjective experience of realizing something, that is, understanding its meaning. The analyst has this experience when he has looked and looked at his patient's apparently incomprehensible material and suddenly realizes what has been staring him in the face. The element which is searching can be thought of as having an unsaturated aspect which, when it meets the appropriate realization, becomes saturated. From a state of being open, like a variable without a value, it develops a value, becomes saturated, and is therefore a constant. At this point it is referred to as a *conception*, row E.

Some pre-conceptions may be innate; for example, an infant seems to search for something on which it can suck, as though it has an inbuilt idea about something like a breast that is available and can satisfy its need. Bion (1962b: 70) states that there is no limit to the number of realizations which can satisfy an innate pre-conception. For example, the pre-conception of the 'breast', an object that will bring satisfaction and relief from distress, can be realized in many different objects.

Having become a conception, row E, the thought is bound, but it can, in its turn, become unsaturated, a new pre-conception, ready to mate with a new but specific realization, and become saturated, or realized. This whole process is that of thoughts growing in complexity and depth, in one direction producing new ideas of greater richness, and in the other increasing abstraction reaching greater and greater overarching principles. This is reminiscent of the description by Matte Blanco (1975) of unconscious sets with progressively deeper sets embracing several of the sets at more superficial levels. Growth both in complexity and in degree of abstraction occurs in the movement through the next three rows.

The *concept*, row F, is derived from the conception by purifying it of anything that would stop it from representing the truth. When something is realized, for example when the analyst recognizes, in the patient's material, something previously unseen, there may be a sense of excitement. This feeling of excitement is not conducive to finding the truth and in fact may prevent it from emerging. Similarly, a wish to find out more and more also interferes with approximating to the psychoanalytic object. These feelings have the effect of blocking openness to experience.

To explain the next two rows, some clarificatory points about science need to be mentioned. Science develops through observation of phenomena that constantly occur together. From these observations, various explanations or hypotheses are developed. These hypotheses can be represented in a system or hierarchy of hypotheses, in which each successive hypothesis is derived from that in the row immediately above it in the hierarchy. This is a scientific deductive system. Psychoanalytic explanations or hypotheses can also be brought together in their logical relationship to form a *scientific deductive system*, row G. From this association, the individual meanings of the concepts are enhanced, for example by being recognized as part of a psychoanalytic theory. Through this process, each analyst rediscovers psychoanalytic theory for himself through his own practice, thus giving it real personal meaning.

As will be explained in more detail later, a scientific hypothesis can also be represented as an algebraic formula or calculus. This much more abstract form means that words no longer have to be used to express the hypotheses; algebraic symbols are used instead. Ideas can then be manipulated without having to be expressed in words. This makes for a far greater flexibility. Row H in the Grid is the *algebraic calculus*, which, as in mathematics, represents the possibility of expressing psychoanalytic hypotheses in an increasingly abstract and generalized form. This allows for the development of increasingly broad generalizations about psychoanalytic principles which might then be recognized in clinical material. The most abstract theory achieved will still only be a derivative of the psychoanalytic object which of itself can never be known.[1]

---

[1] In his notes on calculus formation in *Cogitations* Bion (1992: 49) talks about the need to have signs for 'augments' and 'generates' such as could be used in expressions such as greed, frustration 'augments' envy, or greed, frustration 'generates' hallucinations. Also a symbol or sign for 'of' meaning 'associated with' so as to express frustration 'of' sexual desire in the sense of the frustration being particularized as to the stimulus involved.

The vertical axis describes the development of thought with increased abstraction and generalizability going down the axis from rows A to H. By putting the two axes together, thoughts, interpretations and associations can be located through cross-referencing. For example, the analyst's state of mind in the session is one of free-floating attention. It is an anticipatory state and can therefore be classified as a pre-conception in the vertical axis, and also in column 4, attention, in the use axis, therefore D4. As meaning begins to accumulate, memories from other sessions may enter his mind, column 3, and conceptions may develop, forming a concept which then merges into a theory, rows E, F and G with a cross-reference of increasing probing, hence column 5. With the progression towards making an interpretation designed to have an effect on the patient, there is a corresponding movement down the Grid and from left to right. The interpretation would probably fall in F6 or G6.

The mind of the analyst needs to be in a maximally receptive state in order to be open to the particular experience of the session. Bion's idea of the need for the analyst in each new session to get rid of memory and desire is in order to keep his pre-conceptions from being prematurely saturated. Keeping yesterday's session in mind, or the interpretation that worked last week, or an important dream, all have the effect of blocking the analyst's receptiveness to the new experience of today.

If we now return to the material above of the young man who said that he was now off drugs, this statement could be seen as personal myth and therefore row C, possibly C1 or C3; used to mislead, it becomes C2. His expectation of internal propaganda, his fantasy of what will happen, is again category C, in this case used to discharge unwanted potential thoughts, so C6. The lecture on the corrupt government was an unthinking outpouring of meaningless material, and is therefore row A, the beta elements (see Chapter 7). This outpouring was an action, therefore A6, but clearly it was to block the emergence of any truth, hence A2 (see at the end of this chapter, Bion's concept of a negative Grid). Next is the statement that he had not after all given up drugs. This is the beginning of a developing idea, therefore row D, the combined reference being D4, as he is drawing the analyst's attention to something important. The report of the sexual feeling is a description in words of his experience, therefore row C. The total Grid category is C4, C5, as it has now become a real exploration into the depths of the patient's personality. The interpretation of the analyst is E or F4 to 6, the analyst's conception or concept about the pattern underlying this interaction. Finally the patient's description of watching himself moving away from further insight can be classified as C4, changing to A6 as the meaning is taken out of the interaction.

Taking a statement from a patient such as, 'This analysis is of no use to me'; if this is announced at the beginning of a session, it could be taken as a definitory hypothesis, a definition of the patient's state of mind, hence F1 or G1; G because it might be part of a systematized series of beliefs. It could also be a discharge of what is felt might become a painful state of mind, an expulsion of beta elements by means of muscular action. This discharge may have an effect on the analyst but gives relief to the patient; this would be A6. If the patient feels persecuted and the statement is in the nature of anticipating confirmation of this state of affairs during the session, it is classified as D, E or F, 4 or 5. If its purpose is to elicit action by the analyst such as confirmation or denial, then F or G6. The patient's association may be made for the purpose of denying access to material that would lead to the truth. This would be column 2 and horizontal category F or G if it is systematized.

The Grid is not for use in the immediacy of the session because this would interfere with keeping the mind as open as possible, and free of memory and desire. It is for work on the material afterwards. When a facility has been gained in classifying statements, these categories are automatically noted in the session. As a start, after a session one can try to assign a statement to its use category. To simplify matters, one can first decide if the statement is against eliciting the truth, in which case it is column 2. If however, it is felt to facilitate the progress of the investigation, it would fall into column 3, 4 or 5. Column 6 would be called in if the statement is felt to be an action, a discharge of material or an attempt to elicit action either in the analyst or in the patient. Finally column 1 statements are definitions, hypotheses as starting points, as though to say, 'This is the assumption under which I am functioning today', a statement that seems to define the keynote of the session as far as the patient is concerned or else defines some state for the patient.

The statement can then be classified according to the vertical axis. If it has the quality of the indigestible outpouring of material which does not arouse images, then this is likely to be row A; if it is a state of mind susceptible to dream thoughts or visual images, then row B; or if descriptive of events, day fantasies or dreams, then row C. The statement may be felt to represent an unsaturated element searching for a realization, hence row D or E. If it is a concept or a theory, then row F or G.

The point of doing this is that the Grid is a way of looking at how thinking processes can develop and the mental moves which oppose this development. Bion later thought that to demonstrate those mental processes opposing the development of thought, those under the link of –K, it might be more accurate to have a negative dimension of the Grid which would be identical with the Grid as outlined except for the omission of column 2. This negative mirror image would more accurately describe all the use categories but with a negative thrust, that is, for the purpose of preventing the emergence of the truth. For example, attention would be drawn to some event for purposes of misleading; an interpretation ostensibly would provide insight but in effect would prevent a manifestation of the psychoanalytic object. In other words, what is at present column 2 would he replaced by negative versions of columns 1, 3, 4, 5 and 6. As far as the vertical axis is concerned, the direction would tend to be reversed, from greater degrees of complexity and abstraction towards the emotionally meaningless beta elements.

Although the Grid has been described as it relates to the analytic session from the point of view of both analyst and patient, the whole point of it is that it is a scheme of mental and emotional functioning that applies equally to someone thinking on their own. Intimately related to this are the mechanisms for movement between the categories, which will be described in Chapter 6.

Chapter 5

Myth and the Grid

*We are trapped by language to such a degree that every attempt
to formulate insight is a play on words.*
(Niels Bohr, quoted in Blaedel 1988: 159)

Freud recognized that the myth of Oedipus played an important
part in the content of phantasies concerned with maturation and
sexual development as revealed by psychoanalysis. In Freudian
theory, the whole Oedipus story in its narrative form is relevant
to its content in clinical work. In other words, the sexual component of the story only makes sense in the context of the whole
narrative. Thus there is not only the wish to marry the mother
and to kill the father but there is also the father's castration threats
to his son, just as Laius, threatened by the oracular pronounce-
ment, tried to do away with his son by casting him away on the
mountain. Being bound by the narrative to give them meaning
also places a restriction on the use of the various components in
the story.

In addition to its importance in the content of phantasies, Bion
realized that the Oedipus myth was significant in the development
of the apparatus of thinking. These mythical elements were
precursors of more sophisticated abstractions and theories.
He noted that the various elements of the myth fitted the Grid
categories in a striking way. The announcement by the oracle
about the projected tragedy can be categorized as a definitory
hypothesis, column 1. Teiresias the seer's advice against Oedipus'
wish to pursue the truth fits column 2 as the element opposed to
emergence of the truth. Oedipus, in his attempt to inquire into
the cause of the plague, heedless of warnings against this, can be
classified under column 5, inquiry and probing. Expulsion from

Thebes is the action of column 6. In addition, the notation function of column 3 can be represented by the myth as a whole being used as a record. The Sphinx scrutinizes, asks questions and stimulates curiosity but also threatens death if it is not answered satisfactorily; column 4 represents this.

The myths of Eden and Babel have many elements similar to those of the Oedipus myth. In the Eden myth, God forbids Adam and Eve to eat of the fruit of the tree of knowledge of good and evil. Eve is enticed by the serpent to eat the fruit and she then persuades Adam to do the same. When they do so, their guilt is revealed in that they know they are naked and hide from God. They are subsequently expelled from Eden.

In the Babel myth, the people speak one language. They decide to build themselves a city and a tower which will reach up to the heavens and to make a name for themselves lest they should be scattered abroad. God sees this and says to Himself that they are one people and have one language, meaning that they are united as a group,[1] and this is only the beginning of what they will do; that nothing they propose will be impossible for them. So He decides to confuse their language so that they cannot understand each other, and they are scattered on the face of the earth.

Thus there is, in the Eden myth, the pursuit of knowledge (columns 4, 5), which is forbidden by a god (column 2), who punishes them with expulsion for disobedience (column 6). In the Babel myth, the people state that they are going to build a city and a tower (column 1) and are thus also pursuing knowledge and integration (columns 4, 5) which is again forbidden (column 2) and punished by god (column 6).

These striking similarities and the readiness with which they fit the use categories of the Grid suggest that they are psychoanalytic elements, that is, constructions that have a particular relevance to psychoanalysis, its building blocks, as it were. Their vertical axis classification would be row C. The following can thus be included as elements: an omnipotent god who is hostile to human acquisition of knowledge; human determination to pursue inquiry regardless of the consequences; and the subsequent punishment by expulsion or banishment. There are additional elements such as the enticement to pursue knowledge, which is represented by the Sphinx in the Oedipus myth, who poses a question; if the

---

[1]   They form a work group. See Chapter 12.

answer is wrong, death is the penalty, but if the answer is correct, then the Sphinx commits suicide.

Unlike the sexual value of the myth, which depends for its meaning on the whole narrative link, these elements are related to the processes of thinking and can appear independently in the patient's material. In this case they will bear the individual stamp of that particular personality.

For example, a session in which progress had been made was followed by a dream in which a frightening Gestapo figure was on the same train as the patient, threatening her by saying in a menacing way, 'You'd better be careful, I'm watching you.'

She said she loved an interpretation which she felt had involved courage on the part of the analyst. Later she found herself mocking the analyst for being courageous and felt that the analyst was naïve in 'fighting the forces of evil'. It was better to hide. She had had a dream with a single fruit tree but the tree was covered with ivy, which might sap its strength and eventually cause its death. The fruit tree reminds one of the tree of knowledge in the garden of Eden, the fruit of which God forbade Adam and Eve to eat. Thus there was a force watching her like the Gestapo figure, forbidding any further understanding, and this force was presented as the mocking self. The prohibition against knowledge adds a further dimension to the understanding of the reversal of her pleasure in the interpretation.

Turning now to the Oedipus complex as it is understood in classical analysis, Bion realized that there were some patients who could not understand interpretations about this because they had no Oedipal pre-conception which could meet up with a realization of the Oedipus complex as it manifested itself in their own material. As will be discussed in later chapters, the psychotic part of the personality fears and hates contact with emotional reality and attempts to destroy this by fragmenting particular thoughts, or by a destruction of the perceptual apparatus, meaning that which enables the persecuting psychic reality to be apprehended (Bion). What is destroyed in these ways is the Oedipal pre-conception without which there can be no matching up with the appropriate experience which would enable thinking about the parental relationship to take place. Hence there is no capacity to understand the parental relationship or to reach and work through Oedipal problems. For instance, a woman had perceived her husband's negligent attitudes towards her but was not aware of it. These attitudes had been perceived but had not been taken in. The container, the seat of awareness, had been attacked so that it became sieve-like. There was therefore not the equipment to make a partnership but this deficiency had not been known. Any interpretation made on the lines of the Oedipus complex will not be understood because those elements that go to make up the parental relationship have not been able to cohere so no Oedipal conception has been able to form.

In these cases it might be possible to detect fragments of the fractured Oedipal pre-conception in the material with the idea of putting them together in the patient's mind. Only if this is successful will there be a chance for the patient subsequently to work through her Oedipus complex.

Another way in which the Grid can help to shed fresh light on clinical material is by what is termed negative growth. This does not refer to the negative Grid or column 2 phenomena, but to movement back up the Grid from rows F and G to row C. For example, the various aspects of the Oedipus myth, instead of being used as theories, can be moved back to their place in the narrative of the Oedipus story. We can think of them as characters in a drama. The advantage of this is that it can bring fresh light to a stuck situation by bringing a naïve viewpoint instead of the more abstract theoretical point of view.

For example, the analyst has the repeated experience of making an interpretation which is accepted as illuminating by the patient. Next day, references are made to some other aspect of yesterday's material but the particular interpretation has disappeared. The patient complains about being easily persuaded by others to their point of view and equally has been known to move the analyst around. On other occasions, an agreed fact is turned into a triumph. One has the feeling that although there is a positive welcoming of understanding, there is also a positive wish that clarity should not appear, and that any progress made in this direction will be neglected. Dreams revealed a window with a beautiful view and a blank one with no view. Thinking of the characters in the Oedipus myth, there seems to be a wish to investigate (the open window equals the open eye or mind) like Oedipus, and an equally strong wish to oppose this, like Teiresias. The blank window is like the blind eyes of Teiresias, who strongly opposed Oedipus' investigation because he realized the catastrophic situation that would be revealed. This recognition of the presence of a Tiresias figure who is against the pursuit of knowledge revivified the analytic understanding as to the compulsive need to undo any new recognition and what was at stake if recognition was allowed to develop, namely persecutory guilt and depression.

Other stories which Bion found helpful in providing models for analytic work were those of the tombs at Ur, dated at 3500 BC. The monarch was found buried not only with treasure but also with many members of his court, the assumption being that when he died his courtiers and servants, having taken some drug, were buried with him. The burial site was that of a rubbish heap, so that the townspeople felt that they would sanctify their unwanted objects by disposing of them there. These royal tombs were plundered a mere 500 years later.

The significance of these stories for psychoanalytic investigation lies in the motivation of the courtiers who went to their death with their deceased king or queen, and also that of the tomb robbers. What motivation could be so powerful that these courtiers would willingly give up their lives and what gave the tomb plunderers so much courage that they risked disturbing what ghosts would be expected to be around in such a site?

What motivates someone to turn their back on life, to refuse to look at where blind adherence to their particular monarch, their unquestioned cherished belief, is leading? For example, a patient might refuse to look at any interpretation in case he or she might be influenced by it, and then possibly experience a change of mind. The reason given for this refusal is that he or she does not want to be brainwashed or influenced by anyone.

The motivation of the tomb plunderers is equally important in that they are risking stirring up frightening ghosts of the past, just as the analytic experience also brings back ghosts, terror, guilt, persecution. What motivates someone to take the risk of exploring themselves; is it greed for gain, or scientific curiosity?

The sanctity of a rubbish heap conveys the idea that rubbish will magically be changed into something worthwhile if it resides long enough in the area of the tomb. We think this is a wry joke of Bion's, that a belief that words spoken within the hallowed precincts of psychoanalytic discourse cannot remain as the rubbish they in fact are.

Chapter 6

Container/contained

A great scientific discovery is the recognition of a particularly simple and fundamental form which heretofore had been hidden in a chaos of appearances and misunderstood theories.

(Weizsäcker 1973: 35)

We have outlined in Chapter 4 the different categories that make up the Grid. It is our purpose in this chapter to outline how, on the genetic or vertical axis, developmental movement occurs from one level to the next.

Great systems of thought have frequently stemmed from an insight which has been extremely simple yet profound. A clear example is that of Wittgenstein, whose first theory of language was based on the idea that the structure of propositions corresponded to the way things were related to each other in the real world. This idea had come to him when reading a magazine article about a court case concerning a car accident. At the trial a miniature model of the accident representing the real accident was shown to the court. Upon this was built his theory. From one particular he abstracted a form which had universal application. Such an insight has to be deep enough to support a wide array of apparently disparate facts. While Wittgenstein was reading a magazine article, Bion was listening to a patient saying he could not take something in. Bion said, 'The statement that something cannot be taken in must not therefore be dismissed as a mere way of speaking' (Bion 1963: 6). He went on to say that such words are apposite to the emotional experience and the recognition that container/contained is one of the elements of psychoanalysis. However, such conceptualizations never become concrete in Bion's thinking because he knows that they are themselves imperfect representations of an unknowable reality:

I shall therefore close the discussion by assuming there is a central abstraction unknown because unknowable yet revealed in an impure form in statements such as 'container or contained' and that it is to the central abstraction alone that the term 'psychoanalytical' element can be properly applied or the sign ♀ ♂ allocated.

(Bion 1963: 7)

There is a strong tendency within psychoanalytic discourse for concepts like ego, unconscious or instinct to become concrete. For Bion all such concepts were representations of an unknowable central abstraction. At the heart of the human creature lies a mystery of which all conceptualizations are inadequate representations. Bion preserves this mystery throughout his conceptualizations.

Words accrete to themselves a penumbra of images so in his text Bion substitutes the symbols ♀ and ♂ for container/contained. Symbols, he believes, will have fewer pre-formed assumptions attached to them.

An analyst once had this experience when treating a mentally handicapped man. The patient was aged 33 and went each day to a sheltered workshop where he performed the most menial tasks. The analyst and some of the staff believed that he had a mental capacity that was capable of higher-grade work. In the sessions these words would sometimes dribble out from the corner of his mouth:

I am 33 years old and is that nothing?

And a moment later:

Can't you give me a picture of who I am?

The analyst said:

The fact that you feel they have been thirty-three years of emptiness, waste and nothingness is so painful that it is better to have people's picture of you than to face this ghastly nothingness.

He replied:

Well, if you won't give me a picture what do I come here for?

The analyst stood up, placed himself alongside him and said:

It is like this. There in front of us is thirty-three years of waste, nothing and emptiness. It is like sitting in a train and opposite sits a man with a wounded and diseased face and it is so horrific that you have to hold pictures up in front of you because it is more than you can bear. But the reason you come to see me is that perhaps there is just a possibility that if you have me beside you then you can look at it.

The matter that could not be contained was pain: thirty-three years of waste, nothing and emptiness. The incident is also an image of a mother interacting with the distressed infant in such a way that there is the possibility of the pain eventually being held in the infant's mind.

The archetype for ♀ ♂ is mother's breast/infant. The scene above is of an infant in pain (patient's mind) searching for and being found by the mother's breast (analyst's mind). Bion's conceptualization is that the personality is constituted out of dual elements: ♀ ♂. In this case the patient's mind had not developed the concept of a strengthening ♀ ♂. This is neither a static situation nor one in which the infant is passively being 'held'; Bion's theory is that it is dynamic. There is a ♂ seeking a ♀, and there is an intercourse between the two.

This concept of ♀ ♂ seems to be ubiquitous in the mind and plays an important part in mental development. Our speech contains many examples of inside and outside; 'in analysis', 'acting out', 'in or out of touch', 'getting involved in something', 'being out of one's mind', etc. There is a relationship between ♀ and ♂. For instance the ♀ may be so rigid that it compresses the contents, rendering them static or even depriving them of their qualities. On the other hand, the contents could be so explosive that the ♀ is stretched to or beyond breaking point. With greater degrees of malevolence the result can be mutual destruction. In a loving relationship they can be mutually beneficial. A model of this is the mother with her baby; both can grow through the experience of containing and being contained.

Not only is the personality made up of these two components ♀ ♂ but so are thoughts also. It is possible to break up thoughts into these dual components. There is a ♀ searching for a ♂. There may also be a realization ♂ seeking a container ♀, thoughts seeking a thinker. On the basis that pure thought is non-material, Bion believed that there is a hierarchy of lower-level or embryonic thoughts leading up to that level. At the bottom of the scale are elements which are neither psychic nor material but a composition of both combined. These are the beta elements which form row A of the Grid. Then these basic elements are 'purified' in the sense of becoming less material and more abstract, through identifiable stages.

Bion postulates that the agency that moves the process from one level to the next is ♀ searching for ♂, container searching for realization. The result of this ♀ ♂ mating is a conception, which appropriately conveys the idea of new life with each new development of thought. When mating has occurred at one level, then it becomes a new pre-conception searching for a new realization.

The evolution of thoughts from lesser to greater abstraction and complexity takes place on the model of the ♀ ♂ acting in an emotional environment conducive to growth. Where the relationship takes place in an atmosphere of negativity, the reverse of growth is the result; this is portrayed by the negative Grid (see Chapter 4, p. 44).

The mating of ♀ and ♂ is how mental growth occurs at every stage of development. On the Grid ♀ appears both on the vertical axis as pre-conception and also on the horizontal axis as attention and inquiry leading to action; attention and inquiry being open to further development and in that sense resembling pre-conception. This representation on the horizontal axis re-emerges at each level in the development of thoughts, that is, attention and inquiry are attitudes conducive to finding the appropriate realization.

First it is necessary to explain that Bion realized that giving something a name was a way of binding things together to prevent dispersal, the band around the bundle of sticks or ideas or observations, and nothing more. Having been given a name, however, it was then possible for the meaning of the bundle of ideas to grow naturally and progressively.

As we have said, movement down the Grid represents the growth of thought and this takes place through the pre-conception searching for and mating up with a particular realization, a container meeting up with something to contain and interact with, through which interaction meaning develops.

There are different ways in which the development of meaning can occur when pre-conception and realization come together. First, the coming together can be seen as the saturation of an unsaturated element (the pre-conception) by the appropriate realization. This coming together is a binding together or naming whence further meaning can develop.

In the clinical material above, the analyst thinks that the man has a higher mental capacity than is manifest in his work. In the analytic session, this pre-conception of the analyst's is met with a realization – the patient prefers a picture of himself to the real thing. The question or unsaturated area in the analyst's mind, 'Why does he not manifest his real capacity?' is met with a realization, 'Because he prefers not to know the real thing.' This mating up, the ♀ ♂ in the analyst's mind, is also a naming, for example 'he prefers pictures', which will progressively fill out with meaning as the analysis progresses.

Second, the pre-conception itself can be viewed as a binding together of phenomena as by a name, to prevent their dispersal, and the corresponding realization is what gives meaning to the bound elements.

Again taking the above example: the analyst, standing alongside the patient, is demonstrating, through his action and the way in which he is interpreting, a possibility which is new to this patient, the possibility of an interaction between two people which can result in mental growth. This could be seen as a pre-conception of a container–contained relationship, which, as the analysis progresses, will develop meaning through meeting up with the appropriate realizations.

We can now see that abstraction is not just the extraction of certain more concrete qualities from a phenomenon but it is also the binding together of phenomena which are recognized as belonging together; in this way singling them out from the rest that do not belong. This is what happens when a pre-conception mates with its particular realization. The meaning of this junction then begins to emerge. This is how thought develops; a matching–binding process followed by the accumulation of meaning. The mating up of pre-conception and realization is both an abstraction and a binding of phenomena.

In movement across the Grid, the uses of thought from column 3 onwards increase in their probing capacity, which demands a tolerance of anxiety. This is in conformity with a move from the pleasure–pain principle to the reality principle. This move involves using thinking to tolerate the feeling of frustration engendered by not allowing ready sensuous satisfaction of need, including by hallucination. The denial of sensuous satisfaction arouses rage and resentment which have to be withstood by reasoning and thinking about it. The difference between Freud and Bion lies in the motivation; Freud claimed that the reality principle enabled postponement of immediate gratification in order to achieve a greater measure of pleasure later on, whereas for Bion the motivation lies in the possibility of emotional growth.

What the analyst frequently encounters is either the absence of ♀ or a ♀ that is damaged or porous and not able to hold the ♂, like a muslin bag trying to hold water. Here is an example of this: a patient did not want to come into the waiting-room before the time of the session because if he did he would feel an intrusive child. Emotionally he is an intrusive child but he can't bear to feel it. When this had been interpreted he said, 'I think at the bottom I fear you will leave me if I let you see I am an intrusive child.' So he has the view that the analyst also cannot contain the intrusive child. What we have said here of a thought applies not only to thoughts but also to pain, guilt and regret. There is pain which cannot be suffered, guilt which cannot be endured and regret which cannot be remembered. These are all instances of ♂ but no adequate ♀. There is no constructive ♀ ♂ so that emotional experience cannot be held. When this is the case what explanation does Bion give for it?

Melanie Klein recognized the envious and greedy attacks made on the good object by the infant, resulting in damage and frag-mentation. When ♀ and ♂ are fragmented there is presumably still enough relationship between the fragments to allow some thinking about it, that is, some rudimentary capacity for ♀ and ♂ to interact in thinking. At least the problem can be addressed. But Bion also focused on the interaction between container and contained when envy was a factor. The link here is –K rather than K. Instead of ♀ and ♂ coming together in such a way that results in mutual development, Bion suggests that there is a reversal of the process, so that thoughts become progressively depleted of meaning, through a –K, –L or –H link. There is a greedy or destructive interaction which is a coming together in a mutually destructive way. In this way, too, pain is not suffered but becomes progressively meaningless.

Bion suggests that when the infant projects his fear of death into the breast, he also projects his hate and envy of the undisturbed breast. This results in the breast being perceived as enviously taking the meaning out of the projected fear so that, instead of it being detoxified and fed back to the infant in a manageable form, it is depleted of meaning in such a way that the beneficial meaning of the fear of death, that is, the value of life, is removed but not the fear itself. What the infant then takes back is a terrifying but meaningless fear of death, a *nameless dread*; his fear is increased rather than alleviated.

This is the sort of interaction that is a prototype of the reversal of the thinking process. The ♀ ♂ renders thoughts more destructive but at the same time more and more meaningless, so that ultimately there is a mindless greed and destructiveness. Movement down and across the Grid from left to right is reversed, or there is in place a negative Grid, which renders emotional interaction progressively more meaningless instead of the reverse.

Historical development was conceptualized by Hegel as occurring through a process whereby a thesis comes into collision with its antithesis which then results in a synthesis. The synthesis would then become the thesis in a renewed cycle of the process. Bion formulated development of thought on a model which is not dissimilar. ♀ and ♂ come together to form a conception, but this then becomes the pre-conception at the start of a new cycle. So a pre-conception and realization mate together (hence the significance of the sexual symbols for container/contained) to form a conception. If Bion had no formulation other than ♀ ♂, then growth would not be explained. Therefore it is cast into pre-conception mating with realization to form conception and then the conception starts the cycle again as a pre-conception.

The link between ♀ ♂ may be commensal, symbiotic or parasitic. The parasitic link occurs when the object produced by ♀ ♂ destroys both ♀ and ♂, an example of such an object being incoherence. However, if the incident where this occurs leads to a development of the powers of expression, then what occurs can be seen to be symbiotic, ♀ and ♂ are mutually beneficial. In the commensal link the emotions had served to develop the individual's capacity to invent language forms which then aid emotional development. Therefore the language and the emotions are in an enriching spiral of development. So, for instance, an emotional experience might give rise to poetry and the latter in its turn would enrich emotional development. We shall give examples now of parasitic and symbiotic links.

A row developed between an analyst and a patient where the analyst reacted violently to the patient's apparent contempt for the analyst's rearrangement of times to suit the patient. This led to a rigid stance on the side of both and, for a time, the emotion was so intense on both sides that attempts to express it in speech resulted in angry silence. This exemplifies the parasitic link: ♂ (the emotion) destroyed ♀ (the speech) and the product of the link was angry silence. However, a year later this event was expressed in speech with mutual understanding. Therefore, viewed in *hindsight*, the event is symbiotic because it led to a development in the power of expression. A row can be constructive if, through thoughtfulness, it leads to evolution in emotional communication. In such a case it is symbiotic; if, on the other hand, the outcome is destruction alone, it is parasitic.

Bion examines this structure from another vertex. A new idea bursts into the world through a genius. Bion calls him mystic rather than genius. The mystic has direct contact with God and is God's container. It is then the role of the Establishment to contain the ideas of the mystic and to enable ordinary people to have contact with God indirectly rather than directly. The mystic threatens to explode the Establishment and also the latter threatens to strangle the mystic's new idea by, for example, rigidly codifying it or by idealizing and worshipping it. Hence Bion's wry comment, 'He was loaded with honours and sank without a trace' (Bion 1970: 78). This conceptualization applies to the social group but is also a symbol of the situation within the individual where there is a mystic in direct contact with ultimate reality and an Establishment that contains it or squashes it.

Bion emphasizes the omnipresence of the destruction of the mystic's idea by the Establishment, both without and within the individual, in *A Memoir of the Future*, from which the following quotes are taken.

there are always No-Alls about the place waiting to imprison/deify any thought or idea that causes trouble
(Bion 1991: 135)

The Christians got him [God] in the end; from his messianic prison house he never escaped till every vestige of meaning had been squeezed out of him.
(Bion 1991: 136)

'His [Socrates'] ideas were buried beneath a memorial so deep they could not be heard.

(Bion 1991: 478)

A woman coming from a background of childhood deprivation and cruelty received an interpretation of her tendency periodically to 'throw a spanner in the works' of the analysis with great anger, followed by a feeling of smallness and hopelessness. The interpretation was experienced as a narcissistic blow but in addition it was felt to lock her in, to restrict her development. This was not related to masochism but rather could be helpfully illuminated by the model of container and contained and the institution or deity hostile to development. Thus she could see that it was not so much that she could not bear the wound made in her narcissism by the interpretation but rather the identification of the crushing force with the interpretation that made her feel hopeless.

Another patient's dream revealed her in a group situation in which she felt that the others were either indifferent to her or critical, dismissive and looking for evidence of her destructiveness. An interpretation of this along the lines of the severe superego figure felt to be in her analyst had no effect until it was linked with her feeling that any attempt to express her individuality freely was immediately subjected to a crushing institutionalizing containment, which did not countenance any moves towards individual freedom.

We notice that Bion's concept of container is frequently equated with Winnicott's idea of holding or holding environment. We wish here to differentiate them clearly. Bion's concept differs in three ways. The container is *internal*, whereas holding or the holding environment is external or in the transitional stage between internal and external; the container is non-sensuous but the holding environment is predominantly sensuous; the container together with the contained is active. This activity may be either integrating or destructive, whereas the holding environment is positive and growth-promoting.

Chapter 7

Alpha function

To talk nonsense in your own way is a damn sight better than talking sense in someone else's; in the first case you are a man; in the second you're nothing but a magpie.

(Dostoevsky 1978: 219)

We are now going to look at the first three rows of the Grid in more detail. To do this it is helpful to show how Bion arrived at his understanding of what he terms alpha and beta elements.

The psychotic mind is dominated by elements which, in the neurotic or normal mind, would not be conscious. In addition, the psychotic makes minutely fragmenting attacks on his mind through which an attempt is made to obliterate awareness of his psychic reality, which he hates and fears because of the persecutory feelings associated with it. There is a great resistance to any process, including psychoanalysis, which might integrate these fragments, because the psychotic fears, among other things, that he will then be confronted by a whole, terrifying, savage super-ego.

When working psychoanalytically with psychotic patients, Bion observed that in the splintered, incomprehensible material there were fragments of visual images which were like remembered but undigested bits of sensuously perceived facts rather than complete pictorial images. He wondered if this was merely evidence of the splitting attack on the mental functions or whether it was some attempt to bring together these fragments of visual images to form a whole. Although normally a dream is something that is remembered or described, and psychotic patients do not seem to have dreams, Bion noted that this kind of event, that is, the production of visual pictures, occurring in the analysis of the schizophrenic, was very like a dreaming process occurring in the session; not that the psychotic patient was asleep but that his mental experience was one of seeing visual elements as though they were dream images. To quote from Bion,

> At one point I suspected that my interpretation was being made into a dream. Thus he sees a tunnel with a train in it. The train stops. 'Won't be able to get cured. Too early and since I just missed it there will not be another for a long time. Minute fragments like faeces . . . two chairs and the three-piece suite; stool chair. I can't talk properly.' Then he started on the 'dream'. It was clear to me that a distinction was being made between talking 'properly' and some kind of talking in visual images.
>
> (Bion 1992: 33)

In another example, a psychotic patient sat up suddenly and looked around in a dazed way. The analyst thought that if he were feeling what the patient seemed to be feeling the experience would be more understandable if he, the patient, were asleep and dreaming. These sorts of experiences led Bion to wonder if it was only in the presence of the analyst that the psychotic patient could risk commencing a process that might be a precursor to the so-feared integration. Thus he linked what he described as a dreaming process in the session to the beginnings of the integrating process.

This view of dream-work differed from Freud's which was that the dream, through the dream-work, concealed the unconscious meaning which could only be revealed by analysis of the dream, the undoing of the dream-work. Bion's view was that the conscious and unconscious material was rendered more comprehensible by the dream-work, in the sense that it became processible into elements that could be used for furthering the integrating processes of thought.

The absence of dreams in the psychotic patient suggested that something about the production of dreams contributed to the synthesis of thought so dreaded by the psychotic. Bion then moved on to the idea that there was a process which was *not* occurring in the psychotic part of the personality, of which dreaming was perhaps only a part. Absence or destruction of this process rendered the psychotic patient severely incapacitated in the mental capacities of attention to the wider field of experience, memory, judgement, and in the production of dream pictures and the sort of visual imagery that evokes associations.

This process, which was not occurring in the psychotic patient, is one whereby conscious rational events as well as pre-verbal unconscious impressions are rendered accessible to the personality so that they can be used not only for the integration of thoughts, but also for other functions such as memory. He realized that the psychotic patient was actively attacking this function in order to avoid integration, but in doing so he was depriving himself of the input needed to enable his mind to develop.

The psychotic's contact with reality seems to be very limited. This is the price paid for refusal to allow the integration which would result in the emergence of the painful psychic reality. Bion posits that there is a crucial decision in every individual, whether to evade frustration or to modify it by thought.

We now return to what was *not* occurring in the psychotic mind. To facilitate thinking about this unknown process which he believed had some resemblance to dreaming, Bion labelled it *alpha function* and the products of its action he termed *alpha elements*. Alpha function acts on the data from a person's total emotional experience, which includes those arising out of the sensory input from external and internal sources. It renders this emotional experience comprehensible and meaningful, by producing alpha elements consisting of visual, auditory and olfactory impressions, which are storable in memory, usable in dreaming and in unconscious waking thinking. The latter includes the input into thinking of images stored in memory which add richness to the conscious thought content. By naming it alpha function, Bion hoped to be able to keep the concept open to avoid the premature imposition of meaning. Alpha elements form row B of the Grid.

In a normal conversation a visual image might arise in the mind of the listener in response not only to the content of the material being discussed but also to the total emotional experience of that moment. This visual image is a result of a mental assimilation of the experience which is being perceived sensorially and it can be stored in memory or used in dreams. It is also in a suitable form to become a symbol. The experience has been subjected to alpha function and has thus been rendered assimilable to the mind.

This requirement that emotional experiences need to be processed before they are in a form that can be used by the personality is reminiscent of Kant's view that objects cannot be thought except through the synthesizing categories of the understanding, and that without this synthesis there can be no knowledge of objects. Bion's position on this, however, is based on his experience of psychoanalysing psychotic patients; he is dealing with emotional experiences not with objects in general and he is conceptualizing more primitive phenomena.

A painful emotion, if acted upon by alpha function, is transformed into dream images and then abstracted into thought through the processes described in the Grid categories. If, however, alpha function does not act on it, then the experience is expelled through anxiety-driven activity. A patient said, 'I did not have to get up to go to the toilet in the middle of the night because I had a dream.' She intuitively recognized that something was held by the dream so it did not need to be precipitately evacuated.

Those events that cannot be entertained in the mind Bion called *beta elements*. This name does not confer status but is Bion's way of delineating the raw data that are present. They are sense impressions devoid of meaning or nameless sensations which cause frustration. For example, they may be persecutory or depressive in nature but they are incoherent. They are undigested and feel like things-in-themselves, as foreign bodies in the mind. They are suitable only for evacuation because they cannot be thought about. If persecuting, they feel like debris of which the mind wants to rid itself; according to the pleasure principle, that which causes discomfort is expelled. This expulsion takes place through projective identification into the body, or into the external world. Although this is a mental event, it is described as if it were a physical process and indeed may be experienced as such by the recipient. In his book *Experiences in Groups* (1961), written before he had developed his mature psychoanalytic theory, Bion described the *proto-mental system* which contained primitive data of the mind where the mental was not distinct from the physical. What he later described as beta elements are the raw elements, the content of the proto-mental system. Events arising from this system can be experienced as mental or somatic events.

A woman in analysis had the experience for the first time of being able to generate thoughts during the analyst's absence. Then she experienced regret that she had not acquired this capacity earlier in life. This experience was just a 'glimpse' and it was painful. She then catapulted the pain away. Where to? Into the analyst. She said the analysis was no good, it had done nothing, that the analyst always tried to make out that things had been solved. The analyst felt annoyed and tempted to retort. The impulse to retort was stimulated by the painful but unthought emotion – beta elements – that had been projected into the analyst. These beta elements elicit emotional involvement in the analyst, which may, although not in this example, interfere with the analyst's ability to observe and think. They may achieve this by blocking the searching pre-conceptions of the analyst.

Beta elements, which form row A of the Grid, are not in a condition to be thought about. They cannot be verbalized and are not able to yield their meaning, but they can be transformed so they become suitable for use in thinking, in other words they become processable by the mind. For this to happen, they must be submitted to the unknown process of alpha function; they then become alpha elements which can be used in thinking and in dreaming. Alpha function endows the mind with a sense of subjectivity. Now the mind can think about itself and have a personal response to emotional occurrences. It is able to transform the basic emotional experience into thought. Without alpha function a person can abstract the sensory data pertaining to the external world but not to those of internal emotional experience. Also the person cannot have a subjective emotional apperception of the external world. A philosopher therefore may be able to abstract from sense data but be unable to achieve self-knowledge.

To explore the usefulness of this concept of alpha function in clinical work, it is necessary to look at the material on which it acts to render this material 'digestible' to the mind.

A patient speaks of an emotional state which he is currently experiencing but he is unable to name or describe it, although it is obtrusive and uncomfortable. He does not seem to recognize it as belonging to any category of emotion of which he has heard. He might say that it is unpleasant, that it fills him up, but that he cannot go any further in describing it. Another patient talks of a sensory object or an event, but the description seems to be devoid of any resonance or associations which might, if present, be evocative of images. It is as though the object or event has no meaning, no undertones or overtones. It seems to be undigested. These experiences are examples of the unprocessed data upon which alpha function acts, but they are difficult to define, possibly because the very process that would render them comprehensible, namely alpha function, is lacking.

A patient who contemplated increasing his sessions from four to five experienced acute apprehension. When trying to describe it he said, 'I have often spoken of impressions and feelings that I hate and want to repudiate but this is different. It is just indescribable.' At this moment he pointed to his chest and said, 'It's in there somehow.' The analyst said, 'As if it were an undigested lump that just cannot be processed.' The patient replied, 'Yes, that's exactly how it is.' You will note his words, 'how *it* is'. It is not something of which the patient was able to say 'I feel'. There is no 'I' and there is no separate something in relation to the 'I'. This illustrates why we have said above that alpha function transforms inanimate non-personal phenomena (beta elements) into subjective experience.

One indicator of alpha function is the transformation of the raw data into internal visual images and to a lesser extent other internally initiated sensory images such as occur in dreams, daydreams and ordinary waking thinking, of which the visual image is the most dominant. These comprise row C of the Grid and are used in the description of an event; for example, if we describe part of an analytic session we are merely giving a personal picture of the event, using these row C images.

During sessions with another psychotic patient, Bion thought that he was expected to be either the patient's conscious mind while the patient was the unconscious part, or vice versa, as though both could not be held in the one personality at the same time. He had the experience of feeling sleepy but not being able to fall asleep but at the same time of not being able to stay awake either as though both states, sleep and that of being awake, were being interfered with by elements from the other state. From this he deduced that some barrier, like the contact barrier described by Freud in his 'Project for a scientific psychology',[1] which would normally prevent the elements from one state of mind from interfering with the other, was lacking.

He hypothesized that this *contact barrier* was composed of alpha elements which were not being adequately produced in the

---

[1] The contact barrier between neurones provided resistance to the passage of excitation from one neurone to another. This is now recognized as the synapse (Freud 1971a: 298).

psychotic patient because of interference in alpha function. This contact barrier separates conscious from unconscious mental phenomena. Its permeability allows some interchange between the two but not a swamping of one by the other as occurred with Bion's patient above. It is while this membrane is being produced that there is an ongoing correlation of conscious and unconscious elements which, after abstraction, results in comprehension of the emotional experience. It also allows for storage in memory and for repression.

When someone engages in a conversation, normally he or she is not bombarded with previously unconscious material, the distraction from which would effectively prevent normal communication. The contact barrier prevents this from happening but it also allows enough unconscious phantasy, presumably stored in memory, to percolate through to consciousness, thus rendering the conversation resonant. Without this penetration the interchange would sound very rigid and sterile, evoking a 'So what?' response in the hearer. The contact barrier also allows repression and storage in memory to proceed undisturbed, yet influenced by events from waking life. In the moment of emotional insight there is a conjunction of unconscious and conscious elements.

A mass of incoherent stuff pours out into the analyst as though the patient's mind can only relieve itself by disgorging it. To the analyst it seems both incomprehensible and also persecuting to some extent. There seems to be no relationship between the different words or half-sentences, the material seems dead. To quote again from Bion,

> It means that I am forced to have an emotional experience, and that I have to have it in such a way that I am unable to learn from it. I have consciousness, a sense organ enabling me to perceive the psychical qualities (as Freud puts it in *The Interpretation of Dreams* [1971b], but I am not to be allowed to comprehend it. Then I cannot learn by the emotional experience, and I cannot remember it.
>
> (Bion 1992: 220)

An outpouring of beta elements by the patient has the capacity to evoke or provoke in the analyst particular emotional reactions as opposed to thought. There is no separation of the mental phenomena into conscious and unconscious functions and consequently the material seems confused and often resembles a dream or an hallucination. Beta elements do not allow the formation of a functional contact barrier but they do appear to form a purposive structure which, for convenience, is referred to as a *beta screen*.

In this chapter we have tried to give an indication of how Bion derived his hypotheses concerning beta elements and alpha function from his work with overtly psychotic patients. But a beta element evacuation does not only occur in the overtly psychotic; it is a very common occurrence, and when it occurs there is a change in quality observable in the session. The beta element discharge may sound like rubbish, a sticky mess, or a stream of monotonous material that evokes no images. This is category A6 on the Grid.

The *beta screen* elicits feelings in the analyst[2] rather than thinking which might eventuate in an interpretation, which in turn might get the patient in touch with the reality he hates and fears. The analyst finds himself making a remark that sounds either accusatory or full of banal reassurance, neither of which will get the patient in touch with the nourishment his mind needs, that is, of psychic truth. It is as though the function of the *beta screen* is to stop the analyst from thinking and instead to act out. The definition of an interpretation needs to include alpha function in its conceptualization. The analyst, too, can always discharge beta elements dressed up as an interpretation.

A patient repeated over and over again that when the analysis finished she would neither speak about it to anybody nor would she acknowledge the analyst if seen in the street; she had suffered so much in the analysis but her friends saw it only as an indulgence. This verbal barrage and others like it were resorted to frequently. Initially the analyst had felt irritated or angry, later exasperated, and finally tolerant and curious. It was then possible to see and to say to the patient that this outpouring formed a barrier to interrupt and block understanding. The patient immediately said, 'It's like putting on a record that I play over and over again; then I don't have to think.' Through the interpretation, resulting from the *beta screen* finally being processed in the analyst's mind, the patient

---

[2]   Bion is particular in his use of the term 'counter-transference' in that he maintains the early definition of it being the unconscious reactions of the analyst to the patient's material. He says that nothing can be done about this except analysis of the analyst. In speaking of the *beta screen* he wishes to focus on the contribution of the patient to the analyst's feelings.

could also use alpha function to transform the outpouring into a visual image, which she could then name. The interaction was now experienced as an emotional reality.

Sensuous evidence falls in the category of beta elements which arise from the body, from the so-called proto-mental system where mental and physical are as yet undifferentiated. They thus form the matrix of thought but are not yet thoughts. In his *Brazilian Lectures* Bion quotes a poem by John Donne to illustrate the transitional area between beta and alpha elements, from something that is not thought to something which is: 'the blood spoke in her cheek . . . as if her body thought' (Bion 1990: 41).

When trying to understand how the individual moves from the non-thought area of beta elements to alpha elements which are primitive thoughts, Bion postulated a ♀ ♂ mechanism in which the beta elements might form the ♂. A model for this would be the young infant depending on his mother to process for him his unbearable primitive sensations (beta elements) which he projects into her. The mother does this through her own alpha function. This depends on her capacity for taking inside her own mind the as yet intolerable emotional experience of the infant, for tolerating it, processing it and ultimately giving it back to the infant in a modified form so that it is now tolerable for him. Her attitude of mind in doing this is called her reverie[3] and an important factor in the quality of her alpha function is her love both for the infant and for her husband; the male standing for the principle separating out infant from mother. This interaction of mother and infant, taking place in a loving relationship, is an example of a commensal type of ♀ ♂ resulting in the mental development of both mother and baby.

The most crucial decision on which mental growth depends is whether frustration is evaded or faced. Encountering a painful state of mind, does the individual immediately engage in one or more of the numerous defence mechanisms readily available for the purpose of getting rid of the awareness of the frustration, or is there an attempt to remain open to it, to tolerate it and to think about it?

---

[3] The etymological derivation of reverie is of interest as its present mild connotation of brown study or daydream has wilder origins. It derives from Latin *radix, root*, through *rabere, to be furiously angry*, presumably uprooted in the mind, to the Old French *reverie, rejoicing, wildness*, thence to *resverie, a state of delight, violent or rude language, delirium*, to *rever*, to dream.

At some point, anxiety or another emotionally painful experience is felt to be unbearable. At that moment the individual takes such steps as are felt to be needed to survive. So, for instance, a Jewish mother whose husband was killed in the Warsaw ghetto annihilated the grief in order to survive and protect her baby son. Whatever mechanisms are used, they are directed towards obliterating either the painful feeling or at least one's awareness of it.

Freud's description of the pleasure principle was that of an organism which, on becoming aware of a feeling of increasing psychic tension, experienced as unpleasure, immediately discharged it to achieve again the pleasurable state of freedom from psychic tension. This mechanism occurred as automatically as a reflex response. The muscular system was used to discharge the unwanted build-up of tension, what Freud referred to as accretions of psychic stimuli.

When this evacuative method was found to be inadequate for the satisfaction of desires, the demands of reality had to be taken into account. Freud said that thought developed to be interposed between impulse or desire and action so that there would be available means to act more effectively on the environment to achieve satisfaction. Thought could be used both to help tolerate the frustration aroused by the delay in satisfaction of the desire and to work out some means by which the environment could be forced to yield the desired satisfaction. This was the reality principle.

Bion found Freud's ideas about the pleasure and reality principles, that of the discharge of psychic tension as the primitive means of dealing with frustration, and that of the use of thought to help cope with frustration, very helpful in his conceptualizations about psychotic patients.

The psychotic patient or the psychotic part of one's personality hates psychic reality and therefore opposes any move towards the establishment of thinking. He cannot tolerate frustration and this intolerance does not appear to get modified in the usual way so that he continues to attempt to deal with psychic tension by evacuating it, using the musculature. This could take place, for example, through the expressive movements of the facial musculature, a grimace or smile, or of raising one's eyes heavenwards in exasperation. In a similar way, the accretions could be discharged in a yawn, cough or sneeze, or by evacuation of bowels or bladder. What is evacuated out is the unthinkable emotional experience, the beta elements.

Usually, the 'record-playing' patient mentioned above would pass large volumes of urine before the session, but when she had angry outbursts in her session, she had passed only a few drops. The outpouring of urine was an evacuation of beta elements expressed physically which was interchangeable with the 'record-playing' outbursts, the latter being speech used as a motor discharge of unwanted unthought experience.

As indicated above, the decision as to whether to tolerate frustration over a period of time or whether to evade it is a crucial one for the development of the personality. The word 'frustration' is used here to denote a desire unmet and therefore a painful state of mind which might be, for example, one of depression, persecution, despair, feelings of envy or guilt, acute anxiety, boredom, hopelessness. This is the psychic reality so hated and feared by the psychotic, perhaps particularly the persecutory accusations associated with the idea of a savage super-ego. If there is a belief that this state cannot be tolerated, then an attempt is made to get rid of the pain as outlined above. This means that the personality is deprived of material for thought, that is, material with meaning.

Just as a strand of cobweb stretched between two bushes might suddenly sway into the sunlight and thereby obtrude into the foreground of the visual field, completely altering one's previous perspective of greenery, so may the beta screen suddenly replace the contact barrier during a session. This replacement occurs by a reversal of alpha function whereby the alpha elements of visual, auditory and olfactory impressions are changed back into the equivalent of beta elements, except that now, owing to the change they have been through, the beta elements seem to have some aura of personality, of ego or super-ego, attached to them. In this way they resemble 'bizarre objects', those fragments which are felt to be so threatening and persecutory to the psychotic patient (see Chapter 13).

A woman with a deprived background felt that her sense of deprivation and neglect had been suddenly and deeply understood by the analyst. Then, equally abruptly, she felt persecuted. She claimed that she would not return to analysis because there were microphones in the room and this was why the analyst could remember so much. In this example, the experience of understanding and being understood was immediately followed by a sense of persecution, of something being done behind her back.

This change is an example of a reversal of alpha function. The development-promoting experience, the analyst's understanding through alpha function, is depleted of its meaning, converted into beta elements and projected out, whence they are felt to threaten to intrude back inside the patient; the understanding analyst is now a series of ominous, listening and intrusive microphones. These beta elements now seem to contain traces of menacing super-ego.

In analysis we are attempting to elicit true facts about the personality, so this choice of whether to evade frustration or to modify it is particularly important. Both in analysis and in oneself it is possible to see the moment-by-moment choice as to whether to evade frustration or to tolerate it and on this depends our mental health.

When the attempt to evade frustration dominates, whatever processes render our experience comprehensible (alpha function) are attacked by reversal, minute fragmentation and evacuation by the psychotic part of the personality. In doing so, the psychotic empties his mind but this means that he is unable to utilize his experience. He now feels trapped in his state of mind, having got rid of the means by which he could escape, that is, by thought. His mind is therefore in a state of progressive starvation which may end in a deteriorated psychotic state. During analysis, when an attempt is made to relinquish the destruction or reversal of alpha function, the patient is left with alpha elements but does not yet have the capacity to think.

If a decision to modify frustration by tolerating it is taken, then instead of discharging the undigested beta elements or reversing alpha function, the unpleasant experience is held in the mind in such a way as might render it meaningful, that is, long enough for alpha function to act upon it so that it can be thought. This then has the effect of modifying the feelings of frustration, the thinking process itself, giving some containment of the painful experience, thus making it more bearable.

A female patient had given up smoking. This had precipitated constipation, which distressed her very much. She was also mentally constipated in the sense of not being able to get her ideas out in the session. Her previous orientation had been dominated by evasion of frustration which was implemented through smoking. Giving up smoking, which had caused a prolonged internal struggle, was, in effect, her acceptance of the need for modification of frustration in the service of growth, that is, she was making a stand against the psychotic part of the personality. Following this, she was faced with a persecutory reality, filled with primitive anxiety and meaningless stuff which was felt to be stuck inside her and which she could no longer expel. She tried to discharge this into the analyst by being provocative in the sense of arousing a critical reaction as discussed above in reference to the beta screen. She was in a stuck state, no longer evading frustration but not yet with sufficient alpha function to enable her to think her way out of this state.

In summary, beta and alpha elements are hypothetical entities for which there may be no realization, but they are convenient for talking about something which is in the sensuous realm and therefore not human thought (beta elements), and something that is becoming a thought (alpha elements).

The A6 category of the Grid refers to the discharge of beta elements, an action. As beta elements are not thoughts, the other categories, except for column 2, are not applicable to them. When questioned about the A6 category, Bion said that it

> would represent not thought, but action with actions . . . if no thought were possible the individual would go straight from an impulse to an action. . . . Confronted by the unknown, the human being would destroy it. Put into a verbal formulation of a visual image, it is as if the reaction were, 'Here is something I don't understand – I'll kill it.' But a few might say, 'Here is something I don't understand – I must find out. . . . Here is something that frightens me, let me hide and watch it', or if it became braver, 'Let me go nearer and sniff it.'
>
> (Bion 1990: 27–8)

Something resembling a loss of alpha function can occur when it is necessary to change from one's native language to another by virtue of changing one's country of birth for another country where a different language is spoken. Eva Hoffman, in her book *Lost in Translation* describes her near total loss of identity through the effective loss of language when she moved from her native Poland to the United States of America at the age of 13. All her emotionality was invested in the Polish language and it took many years before English penetrated her deep inner language. This is analogous to a position of being unable to abstract the essential emotional and cognitive elements from experience, including especially the experience of the spoken language. Having dreamed of a cottage which had a powerful source of warmth under its earthen floor, she describes the eventual breakthrough into the English language thus:

> A voice in the dream says:
> 'The cottage is the Heart of Desire; it's the sun itself that stokes the Fire.'
> When I wake up, I understand that words which I would never make up in the daytime, words compressed into metaphor and rhyme, were manufactured somewhere within my sleep. ... English spoke to me in a language that comes from below consciousness, a language as simple and mysterious as a mediaeval ballad, a gnostic speech that precedes and supersedes our analytic complexities. ... I've had English words in my dreams for a long time. But now they break up, de-form and re-form as if they were bits of chromosomal substance trying to rearrange itself. ... But once this mutation takes place, once the language starts speaking itself to me from my cells, I stop being so stuck on it. Words are no longer spiky bits of hard matter, which refer only to themselves. They become, more and more, a transparent medium in which I live and which lives in me – a medium through which I can once again get to myself and to the world.
>
> (Hoffman 1991: 243)

The writer seems to be expressing the development in her of the ability to process by alpha function the English language. The previously 'spiky bits of hard matter, which refer only to themselves' is a description of beta elements.

To end this chapter, here is a quote from Bion.

> Attribution of a value to the term alpha-function is a task of psycho-analysis and can be achieved in no other way. Its status ... is that of an unknown variable to be used to satisfy the need for a system of abstraction adequate to the requirements of psycho-analysis.
>
> (Bion 1962b: 55)

Chapter 8

A diagnosis of thought

*Two things fill the mind with ever new and increasing admira-tion and awe, the oftener and more steadily we reflect on them:
the starry heavens above me and the moral law within me. I do
not merely conjecture them and seek them as though obscured
in darkness or in the transcendent region beyond my horizon:
I see them before me, and I associate them directly with the con-sciousness of my own existence. The former begins at the place
I occupy in the external world of sense, and it broadens the
connection in which I stand into an unbounded magnitude of
worlds beyond worlds and systems of systems and into the limit-less times of their periodic motion, their beginning and their
continuance. The latter begins at my invisible self, my person-ality, and exhibits me in a world which has true infinity but
which is comprehensible only to the understanding – a world
with which I recognize myself as existing in a universal and
necessary (and not only, as in the first case, contingent) connec-tion, and thereby also in connection with all those visible worlds.
The former view of a countless multitude of worlds annihilates,
as it were, my importance as an animal creature, which must
give back to the planet (a mere speck in the universe) the matter
from which it came, the matter which is for a little time provided
with vital force, we know not how. The latter, on the contrary,
infinitely raises my worth as that of an intelligence by my person-ality, in which the moral law reveals a life independent of all
animality and even of the whole world of sense – at least so far
as it may be inferred from the purposive destination assigned to
my existence by this law, a destination which is not restricted to
the conditions and limits of this life but reaches into the infinite.*

(Kant 1956: 166)

We have already seen from Chapters 4 and 7 that Bion was concerned with the generation and development of thought. We want now in this chapter to examine the nature of thought itself. We shall start with a short survey of the philosophical theories of thinking.

THE PHILOSOPHICAL BACKGROUND

Throughout the centuries philosophers and more recently psychologists have endeavoured to think about thinking. Is it an activity involving the whole man, as Aristotle said? Or only a part of man, labelled the mind, or the soul, as Plato thought? Of what does the activity of thinking consist and what are the data on which it works?

Hobbes had said that the content of knowledge derives from sensory experience. Locke said that to this content is added the mind's perception of its own functioning. These supposedly simple units of perception were stored and used in various combinations to produce complex ideas. Locke distinguished five basic operations of the mind: perception; retention, which was subdivided into contemplation and memory; discerning, that is, deciding whether two ideas are the same or different, and on this process depends the capacities for reason and judgement; comparison of one idea with another; and finally, composition, in which simple ideas are put together into complex ones.

Locke viewed the concept of mind sometimes as a container of ideas and at other times as a candle which would illuminate ideas. These ideas seemed to exist somewhere between the objects from which they derived and the mind. That they arose in the context of a relationship between the subject and the object becomes an important aspect of Bion's theory. One aspect of Locke's approach to thinking is a theory in which a series of thoughts are available to be inspected and dealt with by the mind in the ways outlined above. But the idea of the mind as a candle able to illuminate the darkness conveys a sense of a vast unknown of infinite possibilities of which the mind can grasp very little and that only feebly. This latter idea is more in line with Bion's view.

In speaking about communication and language, Locke realized that the vast number of ideas in the mind, the particulars, would have to be generalized in order to make it practicable to speak about them. He used the word 'abstraction' for the process whereby an idea is made capable of representing more ideas than one, that is, those having a common element and stripped of their particulars. When these abstractions are made, they are arbitrary in that they are man-made and for our own convenience. In other words, the abstraction is a variable depending on human choice; it is not a constant with a fixed eternal value.

Locke's belief that thinking is an active process of recognition and assessment is in contrast to the theory of associationism, in which the process of thinking is seen as more passive. It has a history dating back to Aristotle. Basically, simple sensory elements from external reality are impressed on the receptive organism and are linked together into more complex units by laws of association, such as contiguity in space or time, or by similarity or contrast. This theory has application in reflex and operant conditioning, in which the ability to recognize and discriminate is assumed to be a blind response. Association of elements through contiguity, similarity or contrast is a form of mentation that predates thinking or it is thinking in embryo.

Vygotsky (1975) said that true concept formation did not begin until adolescence, but that in children the functional equivalent of concepts, which he termed 'complexes', derived from associative links. Children do not abstract a single trait to form a concept. Although a pre-school child may use the same word as an adult for an object, this is not a concept but a complex of associations. For example, when an adult points out a duck landing on the water, the word 'duck' to the young child means not only the bird but the splashing water, the sounds, the ripples on the lake and so on. These are all the associative links forming a complex. The actual meaning of the word 'duck' has not yet been abstracted. In mature thinking, arising in adolescence, a form is personally constructed or abstracted instead of two objects being linked through similar contrasting shape or colour. Vygotsky said that it is only in adolescence that the individual sorts out and categorizes according to forms or structure, that is, the single attribute that links objects. It is easy to see that Bion, with alpha function lying at the base of his theory of thinking, held a constructivist theory of thinking like Vygotsky. There is a big divide here between Bion and Freud, whose theory of thinking was rooted in the associationist tradition. Bion, like Vygotsky, saw the associationist kind of mentation as a matrix out which thought arises but maintained that it is not thought itself. Each associative element is, in Bion's formulation, a beta element. The philosopher who developed the constructivist view to its peak in contemporary times was Sartre. Sartre was the one who stressed that we are responsible for our own lives, that we construct our lives. It was for this reason that he stressed the faculty of the imagination. Some philosophers had said that the imagination is largely conditioned by the memory traces, whereas Sartre held that it had the power to construct the world almost out of nothing.

The philosopher Hume wrote that in the imagination ideas are connected together by some associative force that is brought into play by qualities of contiguity in time and place, resemblance and cause and effect. When we experience a constant conjunction, the regular recurrence of two similar kinds of events occurring with a constant pattern of contiguity and succession, it arouses in us the expectation that the one (the 'cause') will be followed by the other (the 'effect'). Hume said we cannot derive the idea of causal connection from a constant conjunction but rather that the notion of causality is a projection onto the external world of the natural human tendency to make causal inferences. In other words, after we have observed the constant conjunction a number of times, our minds tend to pass from one object to the other that always goes with it, and thus arises the idea of necessary connection. Bion said the causal inference that we make of events in the inanimate world is a projection into it of a moral category. We suspect that Bion means here a moralizing category as is derived from a paranoid mentality. It is the paranoid mentality which establishes a line of blame. In the human realm we call it blame: in the inanimate world we call it cause. Bion believed, therefore, that the human had been projected into the inanimate. Bion's idea of the human origin of cause and his concept of constant conjunction both derive from Hume.

During the nineteenth century, interest in the unconscious aspects of the mind came to the fore with the study of dissociated states, hypnotism, word association experiments and recognition of the hierarchical structure of both the mind and the central nervous system. For example, Hughlings Jackson observed that destruction of the function of a higher centre in the central nervous system results in the removal of inhibition of a lower centre. In addition, Fechner's theory of constancy gave rise to the concept of a stimulus disturbing the psychological or neurological equilibrium; following this disturbance, measures were required to restore the steady state. Freud based his theory of drives upon Fechner's constancy theory.[1] These ideas influenced theories of thinking in an associationist direction. It is our view that thinking based on associationist ideas is not really thinking at all. In fact a link by association may supplant thought and could be understood as column 2 according to Bion's Grid. We can see also how Freud's idea that there was a causal link between the elements in free association was based on associationism.

Freud's theories of thinking embraced many of these ideas. He believed that the representations derived from external facts as well as those from internally aroused states could be images, ideas, sensations, states of tension and other feelings. He developed the concept of a two-layer hierarchy of thinking: primary processes connected with the unconscious, overlaid by secondary processes in the pre-conscious system. Primary process is again mental activity of the associationist type, whereas secondary process is closer to Bion's model of thinking, thus a metamorphosis occurs from one to the other. Bion investigated this in *Transformations* (1965).

The primary process functions in accord with the pleasure–pain principle; that is, it is based on the need for the organism in an unbalanced state of tension caused by stimulation to return to its previous state of equilibrium. It is rooted, then, in the homeostatic theory. Primary process thinking was therefore based on a reflex model, a build-up of tension giving unpleasure followed by discharge of tension, the relief of which was experienced as pleasure. At this level of functioning, thought and action are the same in that hallucinatory gratification, that is, the conjuring up of the image of the source of relief, could actually, even if only temporarily, relieve tension.

A wish was defined as a current which started from unpleasure and aimed at pleasure; the first wishing was this hallucinatory cathecting of the memory or mnemic image of a previous satisfaction. In the secondary process, the mnemic cathexis was not allowed to proceed as far as perception, that is, hallucination was not allowed. Instead, a delay in discharge of tension occurred by means of thought, until the organism could act on the environment in such a way that the source of gratification was reached. When the ideas derived from thinking became associated with

---

[1]   Today the constancy theory is known as the homeostatic theory, named as such by W.B. Cannon.

words, it was possible for thoughts to become pre-conscious or conscious.

Freud maintained that dreams are hidden wishes using images derived from memories and ongoing somatic stimulation for their portrayal. The mechanisms used in the dream-work such as condensation and displacement make the wish accessible.

Whereas Freud saw thought as a means of reducing tension, Bion, saw it as the means of managing tension. Freud's view that dreams are hallucinated wish-fulfilments is consistent with his view that motivation is governed by the organism's need to reduce tension. This view is not shared by Bion who sees dreams as the process whereby frustration and tension are incorporated and transformed by thought.

Alfred Binet, the French psychologist, was Freud's contemporary although he died twenty-eight years earlier. He began with an associationist model of thinking but through his observational work with chess players, extraordinary calculators, literary writers and children (including his own) he changed his view to one in which emotion became integral to thinking. He held that thinking was dynamic and related to an attitude of preparedness for action. To understand something involves an inner act of comprehension

which no image ... can ever represent. ... One can moreover ... understand without the aid of any kind of image. This understanding ... results from the realization of an attitude, of a particular, indefinable attitude which gives an impression of ease, of difficulty overcome, of intellectual power. ... To understand a word, then, is to feel in oneself the onset of this reaction; ... we are admitting the paradox that one can understand without intellectual realization; one has the feeling of understanding without understanding anything at all; one understands without understanding.

It shows very clearly the gulf separating the two views of mental life; the older view: rational, explanatory, logical, and the other,

a theory of action, according to which the psychic life is by no means a rational life but a chaos of darkness streaked with flashes of light, something strange and above all discontinuous, which has only appeared continuous and rational because after the event it is described in a language which puts order and clarity into everything.

(Alfred Binet quoted in Reeves 1965: 247–8)

This latter view of thinking is one where the mind probes the darkness and glimpses of reality become illuminated. It is based then on a theory of action and bears resemblance to Bion's horizontal axis of the Grid, whose end-point is a probing inquiry and action.

An old approach to thinking was of 'seeing' it as analogous to vision, a series of states derived from the sensory world being passed before the eyes. The linkage of these images in terms of similarity, contiguity in space or time, was the associationist idea of thinking: things being linked through perceptual rather than formal similarity. The action view of thinking is naturally linked to the idea that the acquisition of knowledge is through doing.

Binet, who began from an associationist point of view, came to see thinking as analogous to action or process rather than to structure or state. In this view the mind *is* activity, whereas the associationist view is of the mind as a kind of bag with a whole lot of disparate objects jangling around inside it.

Melanie Klein, while keeping to an instinct theory, developed the idea of a phantasied inner world of object relationships where ego and objects could be split into different parts. She described the mechanism of projective identification in which it is possible in phantasy to split off parts of the self and put them by projection inside another. These projected-into objects become persecutory, threatening to annihilate the ego that expelled them. This gives rise to persecutory anxiety associated with a fear of damage to the self that is characteristic of the paranoid-schizoid position. In this position the ego as well as the object is fragmented. This state of mind oscillates with the depressive position in which integration of self and object has occurred and there is a recognition of a whole ambivalently loved object. The dominant anxiety in this position is that of concern for the safety of the object in the face of one's own destructive urges. One's whole orientation is thereby changed. The ability to negotiate this move from paranoid-schizoid to depressive position is the basis for mental stability. She saw this move from the paranoid-schizoid to the depressive position as not only a developmental stage but also a position which has to be negotiated regularly throughout life. In the depressive position the individual is able to bear pain, regret, guilt and shame rather than to get rid of it. This view, then, is in contradiction to that of Freud because the theory of constancy states that pain is reduced through reduction of tension. The idea that psychic pain is suffered and promotes growth is foreign to Freud's schema.

Bion took up the importance of the oscillation between these positions, which he labelled the PS↔D move, as a crucial one for mental life for a different reason; that it represented the basic mechanism of thinking. It describes the move from a state of formless chaos to that of coherence which suddenly develops through the operation of a selected fact. Thus his emphasis is on the integrating capacity of the selected fact resulting in the Ps↔D move to coherence and the 'spontaneous bleakness' of the truth.

Melanie Klein described how the life instinct leads to the deflection of the death instinct outwards by the infant because he cannot bear it within himself. Bion saw this as intolerance of frustration resulting in the wholesale evacuation of mental contents felt to be unbearable. The persecutory feeling is experienced as a thing-in-itself, not as a thought, and is evacuated mentally with accompanying muscular action.

Melanie Klein's concept of projective identification is underpinned by Bion's concept of ♀ ♂, which interaction leads to mutual development or mutual destruction and depletion of meaning depending on whether the emotional link is K (or L or H) or –K (or –L, or –H). For example, if the anxiety aroused by the projective identification can be tolerated enough to think about it, then a K link is present and therefore the ♀ ♂ is symbiotic or commensal. If however, the feeling cannot be tolerated, a –K link is present and the personality succumbs to the persecutory feelings, because meaning is not allowed to evolve.

Piaget's primary interest was in the development of cognitive structures. He described the two adaptive processes of assimilation and accommodation as major factors in the growth of thought. He saw cognition as a matter of actions which were initially performed on the external environment and gradually interiorized. The more complex intellectual operations were seen as abstracted forms of simpler and earlier operations. He was aware of the intimate relation between affect and cognition. To quote Piaget,

> Affective life, like intellectual life, is a continual adaptation, and the two are not only parallel but interdependent, since feelings express the interest and value given to actions of which intelligence provides the structure. . . .

Personal schemas, like all others, are both intellectual and affective. We do not love without seeking to understand, and we do not even hate without a subtle use of judgment.

(quoted in Flavell 1963: 80–1)

We cannot reason, even in pure mathematics, without experiencing certain feelings, and conversely, no affect can exist without a minimum of understanding or of discrimination.

(Piaget quoted in Reeves, 1965: 265)

Piaget's research endorses the fact that thoughts always have an emotional component and emotions a cognitive one. Bion's descriptive analysis is consonant with this theory of Piaget's.

BION ON THINKING

From Freud's concept of thinking, as being interposed between impulse and action in order to find more suitable outlets for the satisfaction of the impulse, to Bion's formulation implies a big step. Bion points out that thought is now required for thinking about the self and one's own thinking processes; that the apparatus for thinking had to adapt itself for this purpose and it is still at a rudimentary stage, according to Bion, who thinks that the human personality is much better adapted to thinking about inanimate objects as in the pure sciences than about the personality. His view implies that thought was first used by human beings to help master the environment and turn it to human needs and purposes. It is only now that thought is beginning to be directed to the inner emotional experience.

How do we start to become aware of our own processes of thinking? Bion considered it likely that the mental apparatus for thinking developed out of that concerned with respiratory, excretory and alimentary systems. This part of the mind would be aware of the active processes occurring in these systems, those of taking in, breaking things down into basic constituents, discriminating, recognizing and discarding what is not needed. The language we have developed to think about mental processes is frequently based upon these bodily functions. When we apply them to the mind we do so metaphorically. These processes sound much like Locke's basic operations of the mind.

There now arises the question as to the data on which these processes act. In addition to the sensory input from external and internal sources, are there already ideas and thoughts, which require to be thought or does the thinking process produce the thoughts? Although he also finds it necessary to postulate the production at least of primitive thoughts by the thinking apparatus, Bion finds it useful to separate the two, thoughts and the apparatus for thinking the thoughts: 'There are grounds for supposing that a primitive "thinking", active in the development of thought, should be distinguished from the thinking that is required for the use of thoughts' (Bion 1963: 35).

The idea is that there are already thoughts that are 'awaiting' a thinker; consequently the individual has to develop an apparatus for thinking so that these thoughts can be made manifest by thinking them. Using this idea it is possible to focus independently on the so-called 'apparatus' of thinking and its development, but it also conveys a picture of an infinite number of potential thoughts available to the mind engaged in learning from experience.

Using the model of infancy, it is suggested that when the baby is in need of the breast for relief of distress, and has to wait because no breast is present, he experiences his pain as an actively present and depriving breast; in other words, the experience of there being no breast present becomes the positive presence of a cruel 'no-breast'. This presence within him of an absent breast that is felt as something cruel and depriving is a belief that has supplanted the place where a thought 'could have been'. The absence either evokes the creation of a thought or results in a bad no-thing which may then be expelled, which process is registered in the personality as a belief. The thought is like the negative of an object. If one thinks of a tree, the thought occurs because the tree is absent in the mind. Its presence is conjured up by the thought, but this presence is like the negative of the actual object. A patient did not experience the analyst's absence as painful but when she returned after a break she perceived the analyst as an ogre.

Because the baby has a concrete experience of pain and frustration as well as the thought of the depriving no-breast, the latter is felt to be indistinguishable from the painful experience, that is, the thought is the same as the thing-in-itself, the no-breast. At first sight this sounds theoretical and far removed from clinical experience. The truth, however, is the very opposite. We give just this small vignette by means of illustration. The analyst was due to be absent for five weeks. The patient said that it was a relief; he would have more time for his family and could do some extra work in the mornings. Shortly before the break, however, a frightful conflict flared up between him and his partner at work. He had painstakingly written an imaginative literary piece on the word processor. It was poetic in form and had become very precious to him, and his partner had just wiped it off, saying it had no value. He was wounded to the quick and said if he could afford it he would leave altogether. Here was the pain. It was the pain of the absent analyst, the no-breast but experienced in his partner's insensitivity. One has to ask, 'Why was this not experienced directly?' The pain of absence, the pain of a no-breast, if not thought about, is projected into an object which becomes persecuting. In this case the pain was projected into the relationship with his partner. If experienced directly in relation to the analyst, then it is a thought. The analyst concentrated his interpretations upon the patient's pain at the analyst's absence. This no-breast, this painful experience, is a beta element; the painful experience is dealt with by evacuation.

When the breast comes and feeds him, he may experience this as the expulsion of the bad breast. The good breast in his mouth is a concrete object, as is the bad breast which is expelled. But the bad breast, the not-present good breast is different in that it is not associated with a sensuous object. It is a beta element. How does the concrete experience get separated from the thought, the mental representation? We again approach this with a clinical example. A woman gave no sign that she was affected by weekends or other breaks in her analysis but it was a constant phenomenon that subsequent to a break she would become bitter and contemptuous of the analysis. After a few sessions, however, she would become calm and contented. The feed had evidently sloughed away the bad experience of absence. However, it was clear that although she felt better in the calm state it contained bad elements in it: she would be submissive to the analyst despite what he said. It was also evident that when she was bitter and contemptuous she expressed things that were true and accurate, especially certain apt criticisms of the analyst. In the child also to define the absence as bad and the feed as good is to obliterate the possession of objects through thought. It is clear that the resolution of this primitive morality where good and bad are tied to sensuous presence is through a transformation to mental representation.

The problem of separating the concrete experience from the thought that represents it but is not felt to be the thing itself is presumably solved by a process of abstraction; the essential elements are recognized and drawn out of the experience. Something similar must happen in the process of alpha function; the essentials of the experience, the matrix of beta elements, are recognized and separated out from the rest.

One can imagine rudimentary forms of thinking that could only take place in the presence of the actual objects themselves, much as a child might perform simple arithmetical calculations by manipulating actual objects: for example adding three oranges to two oranges to make five oranges. How is the move made to enable the child to think these object manipulations instead of only being able to do it by handling the actual objects?

A baby explores objects by putting them in his mouth or feeling them with his hands. Does the recognition that this exploration can be done in the mind without sensory input occur with a flash of intuition? Freud tried to approach this problem by hypothesizing that when words become associated with ideas, the latter can be consciously thought. This is not an adequate explanation. Vygotsky (1975: 5) believed it was a dualistic error to separate thought and language, that the two were tied together through *word meaning*. He says that word meaning is an act of thought in that it gives a *generalized* reflection of reality but at the same time it belongs in the realm of language.

The baby needs the breast; the patient needs the presence of the analyst. At what point does the baby possess the mother through a mental image and when does the patient possess the analyst in thought? At what point does the baby's desire for the breast pass from satisfaction of hunger to greed? And at what point does the patient's need for the presence of the analyst pass from need to passivity? At what point does the patient begin to generate thought himself?

The foundation of thought lies in an absence. The thought itself has a constructive function; it creates the basic elements of experience into a meaningful pattern. Beta elements are then the basic elements of an absence. However, the only way in which this can be emotionally registered is through painful persecutory ideation whose 'bits' are beta elements. As thought has a constructive function, the root of it lies in alpha function, which transforms persecutory ideation into a meaningful pattern.

Chapter 9

Psychic reality

Anyone who is not shocked by quantum theory has not understood it.

(Niels Bohr, quoted in Davies 1984: 100)

The genetic (vertical) axis of the Grid is concerned with the process of extracting the form from a sensory/emotional experience. This chapter contrasts psychic reality with sensory reality and gives an introduction to the process of abstraction and the models we use in describing our emotional experience.

Science is based on observation and experiment. It attempts to establish hypotheses, which are statements about a constant relationship observed between certain objects or events with which that particular science deals. Later, it may be discovered that the hypothesis established is one example of a generalized law. For example, Copernicus realized that planets move around the sun, and Kepler that the movements they described were elliptical. Newton observed that all bodies fall towards the earth at a uniform rate of acceleration. These were two hypotheses, each stating that certain facts regularly occurred together, that is, the hypothesis described a constant conjunction. It was then realized by Newton (and also by Hooke) that these were both examples of the same law, that of gravity. This generalization of facts takes place by abstraction of the essential relationship between the objects observed; in this instance, the force developed between two masses. The law is an abstract version of the hypothesis derived from the observed empirical facts.

A law is an explanation of phenomena; it does not cause them. Einstein recognized that gravity was not the ultimate force but that it was related to the curvature of space; in other words, gravity then came under an even more generalized law.

Abstraction enables us to deal with things in general, rather than having to deal with many specific concrete examples; this greatly facilitates the task of thinking. It can then be seen whether a particular abstraction can shed light on examples other than those from which the original abstraction was derived.

For the most part, science deals with observations of inanimate data, even when the subject is live; for example, measurements are made on how long a drugged rat in a water-tank takes to find a submerged platform, or how much time elapses before the baby's imitation of the mother's facial expressions diminishes in frequency.

It is the emotional life, the inner being, that is being considered in analysis. The reality or psychic quality we are dealing with can be intuited through the live interaction between the two persons in the analytic situation. This process cannot be described adequately in the language applied to inanimate objects and yet this is all we have. It is significant that the language we use for psychic reality is all analogous. We do not know how, or if, our apprehension of this psychic reality comes through the usual sensory channels, and if so, by what means we understand it. Love, hate, envy, even anxiety cannot be described in terms of the sensory input, and, although changes in heart-rate and blood pressure can be observed, for example, in anxiety, this tells us nothing of the emotional content. Bion says that it 'is helpful to postulate sense impressions of an emotional experience analogous to sense impressions of concrete objects' (Bion 1962b: 55–6).

The vocabulary and the models we use derive, for the most part, from inanimate objects and therefore give a misleading idea of the psychic reality being addressed. For example, in this book, we use words like 'saturation', 'container', 'link', 'crystallization', 'internal objects', which all derive from inanimate objects. This tends to create in our minds a physical picture of the psychic world which is very misleading. The matters with which analysis deals are not apprehensible by the ordinary senses. Words derive from a sensuous background and therefore are not suited to the analytic pursuit but nevertheless have to be used. Analytic terminology quickly loses its vitality and becomes mechanical because of this inadequacy. The language of poetry and of art convey an idea of what is required in the transformation of an emotional experience into a communicable medium.

There may be a common-sense view that everyone knows what is meant by the terms 'love', 'hate', etc., but what it is that constitutes the difference between them can only be apprehended through psychoanalysis. Bion emphasized that this was a very defective instrument but that in the current state of knowledge there was no other. When the microscope was invented it exposed new facts not apprehended before; however, the electron microscope enabled scientists to perceive much more. Let us say that psychoanalysis is equivalent to the microscope; in the future someone may discover the electron microscope. When the emotion is actually present in the analytic situation it is possible to see what constitutes it; what it is that differentiates love from hate or envy from admiration. Although through common sense everyone 'knows' the difference between love and hate, yet the scientific difference is not known.

Freud said that in order to deal with reality, the organism had to develop thought; that the immediate discharge of unpleasureable elements had no potential for fashioning our reality. Human beings fashion the world, both human and inanimate, to their purposes. Within the human being the source of his or her constructive activity is thought, whose root, in Bion's thinking, is alpha function. So thinking developed to be interposed between impulse and action. Without awareness of emotional experience the psyche is starved and does not develop but instead deteriorates, as is seen when psychotic processes continue without remit. Interference with this process of becoming self-aware of an emotional experience occurs not only in the frankly psychotic patient but also in the psychotic part of the personality which can be assumed to exist in all of us to a greater or lesser degree.

Alpha function is that action in the non-psychotic part of the personality that, in some way, enables the distilling out of that essential aspect of the emotional experience which is necessary for emotional development.

To think about our thinking and our emotional experience we form models. In a similar way, to give meaning to what she observes, the analyst forms models of what she thinks is happening in the analytic relationship. This process of model-making occurs through the simultaneous correlation of conscious and un-conscious data as described under the term *contact barrier*, a sort of binocular vision. These models may derive from any aspect of life and provide analogies of the situation as the analyst perceives it. For example, abstractions of the emotional experiences associated with digestion are applied to thinking about our own thinking processes, which are often expressed in the same terms that are used for digestive processes; such terms include: taking in material for thought; chewing over a proposition; swallowing a statement hook, line and sinker; digesting and absorbing an idea; or undigested facts.

Models can be derived from any field, for example from infancy and childhood, chemistry and physics, and from other body systems: excretory, respiratory, reproductive and so on. A model is a concrete analogy of a relationship we are trying to describe. It therefore creates a vivid image and can be easily understood.

A middle-aged man, Mr G, repeatedly interrupted his flow of talk with self-interpretative remarks which usually consisted merely of a direct transposition to himself of what he had just related about someone else. He began his session by saying that a colleague at work had attacked his report that he had spent so much time on during the past few days. He continued quickly, 'I know I'm attacking you and your work.' This sounded bland and somewhat insincere. He agreed that he had thought the analyst must be thinking that too and that he wanted to get in first.

The analyst's model for this was of an intrusive third party, acting as a go-between who interfered with the message. Another model would be a little child wanting to believe that he is helping his mother to feed the baby by taking control of the breast.

A patient may come to analysis because he is stuck in his model-making or because the models he forms of his emotional life are not such as to promote mental development. Phantasies may express these failed models. Model-making also occurs in dreams.

Mr G had this dream following the session mentioned above. He had just moved house to a more fashionable part of London and was returning to his old lodgings to pick up a telephone answering machine. He thought that his two old landladies would be sorry to see the machine go but in fact they were only too happy to help him to remove it. The machine was large and looked rather like a sewing-machine or photocopier. It was clear that the machine was his dream model of the process that interfered with the contact in sessions. It not only came between but was his way of sewing-up the material into a garment of his choosing rather than hearing something less flattering from his analyst. This vivid model is helpful in adding these aspects of the sewing-machine and photocopier, the latter referring to the quality of merely repeating what he has said about another and applying it unchanged to himself. The dream also shows that the previous session had enabled him to separate from the analyst, represented by the two old landladies.

Many models derive from myths which originate in society and are used by it. The Oedipus myth has played a large part in the development of psychoanalytic thought and models from this myth remain vibrant. The separate elements of myths may be more important than their total story, for example the character of Oedipus in pursuing the truth despite warnings against this, followed by his need to blind himself when the truth is revealed.

Models express matters in concrete imagery and often imply causal links between one event and the next. The advantage of the concrete quality of the model is that it brings a sense of reality and vividness back to something that may have become too distant from its roots, but it has a disadvantage in that it may be too concrete, too physical to represent accurately the reality we are trying to comprehend.

We therefore also need to resort to processes of abstraction whereby the essence of the relationship is distilled out. This abstraction must be capable of representing accurately not only the model but also the relationship expressed in the original emotional experience. Initially, the abstract version may be more difficult to grasp but it is more accurate and describes particularly the relationship between objects rather than focusing on the detail of the objects themselves. Later the abstraction may be seen to be capable of representing other emotional situations and can thus be generalized.

An abstraction from Mr G's material above would be: interference in constructive interaction. The examples of the digestive system given above are vivid concrete models; one can almost visualize the thoughts being chewed, broken down into smaller units, which are then absorbed into a larger structure to be used as building blocks. An abstraction from this which would then have wider application would be an interaction between a container and its contents resulting in growth. It is the nature of the link between objects that is the abstraction. The link described in Mr G's material is to interfere with emergence of the truth.

A patient, Mrs A, brings two dreams shortly before a holiday. The first dream is essentially of being able to scavenge, from an abandoned situation, enough material to survive. The next dream is of being in a lift that suddenly drops down to the next floor. Interpretations about infantile feelings of being dropped but being able to survive elicited material about adopted babies and mothers' continued anxiety about them. She sits up suddenly, but to an interpretation about her need to sit up so she can keep an eye on things in order to feel held, she responds by speaking of her cousin who came and sat the patient's baby son up on his own, which, in fact, he could manage. She herself had not thought to try this before; she had not thought that he would be able to. This clearly referred to the patient's feeling that she had greater inner strength than she was being given credit for by her 'anxious' analyst. The analyst had a memory of a pregnant woman who, although she could have been told, did not want to know the sex of her baby before the birth. This visual memory of the analyst's, itself a model, gave rise, on abstraction, to the idea not only of an increased ability to tolerate waiting associated with the mother's increased awareness of her baby's competence, but also of waiting with a pleasurable sense of anxious anticipation, rather than needing to know prematurely in order not to be taken unawares. The dream of scavenging enough to survive was a denial of the real capacity to survive. A further abstraction would be the idea of trusting the absent object. The patient was here showing that she had a greater capacity than her analyst had been led to think for tolerating the state of not-knowing and thus of separation. Here a model was precipitated in the analyst's mind which enabled the essence of the material to be understood. This could then be abstracted into an interpretation about increased tolerance related to an increased inner strength.

The abstraction can be generalized, that is, it can be applied to many different analytic situations, whereas the model, through its concreteness, is much more restricted in its application to other situations.

A model may be too close to the actual experience for it to be effective in rendering it emotionally tangible. For example: at the beginning of a session for which he has arrived five minutes late, a young man says that the traffic was heavy because it is Friday. Using this as a model, one might say that there is also internal traffic in his mind related to the weekend interruption which makes him late for his session. While this might be useful once in the analysis, repetition would not be helpful because it is too close to the actual statement of the patient. Next he falls back on criticizing his father, who, he believes, controls him excessively. Many sessions and much time have been devoted to this topic despite multiple attempts to interpret it. This is the real traffic interfering with him having analysis. It is not the content of the material about his father but the fact that slipping back into it prevents real contact between patient and analyst. The perception of this 'traffic' arises from the analyst's experience in the session of feeling blocked in the attempt to get through to him.

The solution to the model that is too close to the actual experience is either to abstract it further as in this example, where the analyst, through experiencing a barrier to getting in contact is enabled to see the ubiquity of the process of blocking, or else to find a fresh model.

In the clinical situation, the abstraction from the model is used in an interpretation but a model itself or another model derived from it can be used as well to provide a more tangible illustration of what is being described in the interpretation.

Thus, in the clinical example of Mrs A, an interpretation using the model almost directly would be that, like the baby able to sit up on his own, she had more internal strength to cope on her own than had been recognized. In addition, using the other model, one could interpret that she was now able to wait rather than needing to intrude in order to find out, like a mother not needing to know the sex of her baby before the actual birth. Further interpretations based on abstractions from the model might be about the change in attitude from needing to know, by getting inside the analyst's mind, to one of being ready for the risk of being separate and learning through having a new experience. A further abstraction is that learning comes through experiencing a situation as a separate individual rather than through the analyst's eyes.

When we make an interpretation are we just exchanging concepts or is there a realization that applies; are we doing anything more than just ingeniously manipulating symbols? Does the patient really get in touch with something so that light dawns, does he have an emotional experience that changes him, or does he merely learn a new vocabulary so that he can talk about himself in a different way but has had no real emotional experience in the analysis?

Chapter 10

The growth of thought

Through the window I see no star:
Something more near
Though deeper within darkness
Is entering the loneliness.

(Ted Hughes 1982: 13)

THE SELECTED FACT

The material of an analytic session includes statements of the patient and the analyst's perceptions of the patient together with his own experiences, past and present. The analyst produces models out of the elements that he experiences as significant in the material arising out of the current interaction between analyst and patient. This model crystallizes out of awareness of what Bion termed the *selected fact*. This is a particular fact that suddenly occurs to the analyst which makes sense of the disparate elements previously noted. What before may have been a jumble of fragmented material now becomes unexpectedly coherent and understandable; meaning suddenly dawns. This selected fact was described by the French mathematician Poincaré when he said,

> If a new result is to have any value, it must unite elements long since known, but till then scattered and seemingly foreign to each other, and suddenly introduce order where the appearance of disorder reigned. Then it enables us to see at a glance each of these elements in the place it occupies in the whole. Not only is the new fact valuable on its own account, but it alone gives a value to the old facts it unites. Our mind is frail as our senses are; it would lose itself in the complexity of the

world if that complexity were not harmonious. ... The only facts worthy of our attention are those which introduce order into this complexity and so make it accessible to us.

(Poincaré 1952: 30)

A male civil servant of high rank was pleased at himself for his skill in chairing a difficult committee. He went on to say that he felt more confident about his life in general and that of course he realized that these improvements were due to the analysis. The analyst did not feel moved by any of this, in fact he felt superfluous. A song started up in the analyst's mind, and, after groping for them, the words were found to be, 'The king was in the altogether', which was from a musical version of the story 'The Emperor's New Clothes'. Here, then, was the selected fact which shed light on the patient's prancing around in a superior state of mind but at the same time needing a voice, like that of the child in the story, to call out, 'But the emperor has nothing on'.

The patient felt brought down to earth and relieved at understanding this. The above example shows how an image in the analyst's mind illuminated the meaning of the session but also how the analyst in turn realized that this selected fact threw light on a much more general situation, applicable to work with other patients, namely of being like the emperor's courtiers in going along with the emperor's (patients') point of view rather than seeing the situation from an independent angle. The insight illuminates not only a characteristic about that particular patient, but also the form which is thereby abstracted from the material is applicable across a range of phenomena.

This is another example of the selected fact: a patient who came twice a week was in crisis so the analyst offered him a session on the following day. The patient was amazed and felt cared for, that the analyst had concern for him. Then he said that he had a thought he did not want to voice: that the analyst had said this because he wanted the money for an extra session. Two days later he asked for a change of time on a particular day but he said it in stealthy way. Awareness dawned and the analyst said to him:

The thought of two days ago that I offered you an extra time for the extra money has now become a delusional conviction. On Monday this was just a thought but by today it has become a belief, a passionate certainty, that has to be checked out. If

I have a lot of free times, then my practice is depleted and I am offering you extra sessions for my own greedy purposes. We see, I think, why you had an inhibition about voicing the thought: that there is a knowledge inside you that such a thought grows into a paranoid conviction.

The analyst thought further on this matter: that the inhibition in giving voice to a thought is due to an unconscious knowledge that it degenerates into a delusion. Further thought allowed the analyst to conceptualize that the inhibition in expressing the thought was because it was not a thought but a delusion. This insight was a selected fact that illuminated other inhibitions not only in this patient's behaviour but also in that of other patients: that an inhibition in expressing a thought is because it is a delusion. In other words an inhibition is a mechanism for concealing a delusion. This selected fact illuminated not only a reality in this patient's character structure but also a feature of mental life that can be observed in other patients and in social life generally.

Melanie Klein defined the basic psychic move from the pain of persecutory anxiety, when danger seems to threaten the self from a fragmented psychic world, to depressive anxiety, when anxiety is felt on behalf of the object which is now experienced as a whole object, but endangered by the destructiveness of the self. She referred to this as the move between the paranoid-schizoid and depressive positions, oscillation between which occurs throughout life, but mental health depends on the ability to move into the depressive position. Bion referred to this as the move PS↔D. He became aware of the relevance of this shift to the process of thinking, namely that thinking consisted of a move from a formless state where images and ideas are dispersed and chaotic (the PS state of mind) to a state where coherence becomes manifest and a new understanding is realized (the D state). This means that every understanding takes place through this move (PS↔D) from incoherent and scattered ideas to a new synthesis.

Movement down the Grid takes place through the repeated mating of realization with pre-conception, the resulting conception becoming the new pre-conception. In other words, to move from one Grid category to another, a state of incoherence is reinstated following which a new integration takes place. This is the PS↔D move.

The selected fact is such because it is a common meeting point for many different hypotheses held about the particular aspect of the psychoanalytic object being considered. Thus a number of selected facts could be combined and, with further abstractions and combinations, could form a system of psychoanalytic theories (a scientific deductive system) which would further illuminate the psychoanalytic object.

In the sciences, the scientific deductive system is a hierarchy of scientific hypotheses which are *logically* related to each other; each hypothesis being logically derived from the one in the row above it in the hierarchy. This is like a family tree. The hypotheses at the top are the most abstract, for example laws, and these more abstract hypotheses act as premises from which hypotheses in successive rows are drawn. Confirmation of one hypothesis goes some way towards proof of hypotheses at the same level.

We have mentioned scientific deductive systems in psychoanalysis. How do these differ from those constructed in the sciences? In psychoanalysis we form models (see Chapter 9) from observations made of the interaction during the session. Abstractions from these models make up lower-level hypotheses in the deductive system. With further abstraction, new analytic theories are derived or else it is realized that the abstraction made from the observation fits an already existing theory. Theories form the higher levels of the psychoanalytic scientific deductive system. In such a system, however, the relationship between the elements is not logical in the sense of implying causation. Psychoanalysis is about the underlying patterns that reveal manifestations of the psychoanalytic object. The relations of elements in the object has nothing to do with logic.

Science, for the most part, deals with inanimate objects, and even when the objects of study are animate, it isolates measurable inanimate factors for observation; whereas psychoanalysis deals with an evolving process to do with the growth of the mind, that is, with developing thoughts and thinking processes, in which the idea of causation misleads because it blocks understanding of the process. Although the sudden realization, occurring when the selected fact precipitates a coming-together of facts, does give the appearance of being caused, these facts are contemporaneous so that time and therefore causation are not involved. The object of the sudden realization is a *form* which links heretofore disparate elements.

The patient's narrative conveys an idea of causation. Psycho-analytic understanding, however, is related to the development of coherence in a previously incoherent collection of facts and is associated with the emotional movement from the paranoid-schizoid to the depressive position, precipitated by the crystal-lization of the selected fact. The crystallization of coherence is a sign that there has been a PS↔D move and a clarification of the psychoanalytic object. Therefore what the patient may believe relevant to the analytic investigation from the causative elements of his own narrative is unlikely to be relevant to the discovery of the selected fact.

It is worth noting here that Bion was aware of the extreme limitation of the human capacity for thought. He makes the point in later works (Bion 1991: 85) that the fact that we see events as succeeding one another in time or as following certain patterns or laws may be due merely to the peculiarity of our way of thinking. He regards the idea of causation as fallacious and having more to do with the desire of the analyst for a peaceful state of mind; it rationalizes and thus hides a sense of persecution. Applying thought to emotional experience is still at an embryonic stage of development.

THE PSYCHOANALYTIC OBJECT

Science develops through the observation of phenomena that constantly occur together. For example, a stick in water appears bent, bodies of different masses fall with the same acceleration and the volume of a gas decreases as the pressure increases. These observations concern the relationship between interdependent properties or variables. Descartes realized that it would be possible to represent relationships between two correlated vari-ables in a visual form by points in relation to two axes at right angles to each other. Thus each point would represent the relationship of the two variables, say x and y, and these points could be joined to form a graph.

But if variables could be represented on a number plane, then geometrical figures could equally be represented by algebraic equations. By subjecting geometry to algebra it could be freed from the constraints of the visual sphere. This revealed, for example, that the essence of geometry, the true basic objects of geometrical thought, did not consist of points and sections of straight lines but rather of straight lines extending infinitely in both directions. In other words, the configuration underlying what was apparent on the surface was a much more all-embracing one.

What has this to do with psychoanalysis? Bion saw the personality as being composed, not of structures such as are implied by the terms ego, id, super-ego and the unconscious, but as a series of functions, of variables in relationship to other variables. As a common-sense example of this, we quote Whitehead, 'His temper is a function of his digestion'(Whitehead 1958: 107), that is, he transfers onto external situations that relationship which exists between his meal and his stomach, for example a mutually bruising one. We can observe his irritability and the way in which he gets into a bruising relationship with his colleagues. The quality of a function depends on the sort of attributes or factors of which it is composed. These attributes can be described by certain analytic theories. For example, anal erotism and sadism are factors contributing to the function of speech in a particular personality, indicating that the speech shows a mixture of a tight-lipped quality together with a profuse outpouring of dead material. The combination of these different factors leads to the individual differences between people, so that the quality of a function such as alpha function will vary between different people.

His temper is a function of his digestion. Distance moved is a function of time. y is a function of x. These sentences describe the relationship between two variables. While Bion does not wish to be tied strictly to mathematical definition, he does wish his use of the terms, such as variable and function, to retain something of the mathematical meaning. He looks at thinking in the light of relationships between variables. He sees the mating of pre-conception with the appropriate realization as being the saturation of an unsaturated variable, that is, giving it a value, a meaning, thus making it into a constant. But it remains a constant for only a very short time before it again becomes unsaturated to form a new pre-conception. If the latter process does not occur so that the conception or pre-conception remains saturated, its value remains fixed and the concept can develop no further; the idea therefore becomes entombed. The illuminating interpretation becomes a dogma. The following quote gives an example of the variable being turned into a permanent constant, that is, god becoming God: 'Whether scientists or priests, they are restricted

by the human mind which clings to ideas such as god; the variable is substituted by a constant and then venerated as Constant'
(Bion 1991: 414).

Bion uses the term 'psychoanalytic object' to indicate what
psychoanalysis is about, what it aims to clarify. Progressive manifestations of the psychoanalytic object evolve in the course of the
analytic relationship. If both members of the couple are open to
it, it will contribute to growth. The mechanism of this growth of
thought is the pre-conception, which is comprised of a constant
part and an unsaturated part which is searching for saturation.
Bion designates this as ψ (ξ), (ξ) standing for the unsaturated
aspect. The nature of the saturation process is not known, but ψ
(ξ) stands for a complex series of ideas. Of the psychoanalytic
object Bion says:

> Its most extended form suffers from requiring the whole of
> psycho-analysis, past, present, and future, for its expression and
> elucidation. Its most economical formulation is incomprehen-
> sible without experience. [It] represents a constant [with] an
> unknown component, a variable, an unconscious which remains
> unconscious, a source of speculation and disturbance.
>
> (Bion 1990: 11)

For example, one might observe that a woman seems lively and
is often laughing. This is an outward manifestation of what can
only be investigated psychoanalytically, the psychoanalytic object.
Under such investigation, the above observations may be revealed
as the outward manifestations of a state of sadness which has been
revealed in a sudden crystallizing awareness in the analysis. A
saturation has occurred leading to this awareness. But this is not
all. As the psychoanalytic object again becomes unsaturated, a
further revelation is that the sadness is related to the inability to
love. Further clarification of the psychoanalytic object in this way
occurs as a new state of unsaturation is established following a
saturation with its accompanying crystallization.

Growth in thought occurs by progressive abstraction and generalization. Descartes revealed that one mathematical form, geometry, could be expressed more abstractly in another form,
algebra. Through this step, mathematics made a great leap forward
in increased ability to manipulate ideas. Bion had the idea that
progressive abstraction in the growth of thought might result in
a similar breakthrough in our understanding.

CONSTANT CONJUNCTION

The term 'constant conjunction' applies when a number of facts or events are seen regularly to occur together. Once this constant conjunction has been observed, it can be named and can then establish itself as a psychological fact. The name binds the elements together. If it is not named, one is liable to lose track of it and its elements become dispersed. The name means only that these facts constantly go together. It has nothing to do with cause and effect. A concept can be built up in the mind by means of noting a constant conjunction. Once a constant conjunction is named, it begins to accrete meaning. The named constant conjunction is one of the facts that may come together and be given meaning with the emergence of the selected fact.

An analyst noticed that whenever he made a mistake the patient became very excited. There was a constant conjunction between these two and when named 'gleesome error' they became a unitary phenomenon, the meaning of which gradually developed.

Movement down the vertical axis of the Grid occurs through a pre-conception mating with a realization. The conception thus formed is a reformulation of the growing concept. It is also a naming, and, thus named, the experience is saved from dispersal and its meaning can begin to accumulate. This process is repeated with increasing growth in richness of meaning.

As a model of the development of a concept through the constant conjunction of elements, Bion gives the example of how an infant might develop the concept of 'Daddy'. The infant begins to associate the term 'Daddy' with a group of experiences; seeing a particular figure who has a unique sound and smell, a sense of wanting him and of being loved by him, of seeing him with Mummy and of hearing his mother repeatedly say in the presence of this person that this is Daddy.

This is an emotional experience and it is from this setting that the infant abstracts certain elements which for him represent 'Daddy'. This name is applied whenever these same elements are seen to occur together, that is, whenever they are constantly conjoined. The infant in this imaginary situation has constructed an hypothesis. He has observed that certain elements are constantly conjoined and he has named this hypothesis 'Daddy'.

When the infant meets another man who is also called 'Daddy' but is clearly not the same man, he can either give up his hypothesis or adapt it to accommodate the new experience, which clearly has some elements in common with his original experience but in other ways differs from it. In this way a hierarchy of hypotheses can be built up from his various and expanding experiences all labelled 'Daddy'. This hierarchy of hypotheses called 'Daddy' is a scientific deductive system, and provides a richer meaning to the concept than any one hypothesis on its own. It enables the concept of 'Daddy' to be generalized.

The term 'Daddy' could apply to any one of the following four different entities of which the first is the thing as it is supposed to exist in reality, that is, the *thing-in-itself* which is essentially unknowable.

'Daddy' is also the name given to the *selected fact* which precipitates the awareness that the facts are related. The infant suddenly becomes aware that all these observations: the sight, smell, sound, love for and of this object and the sound of the word 'Daddy' all go together to make the hypothesis.

Third, 'Daddy' is the name given to the *facts which are brought into coherence by the selected fact*, the group of abstracted feelings and ideas in the mind as outlined in the previous paragraph, which are seen to be related to each other.

Finally it applies to the hypothesis or *hierarchy of hypotheses which states that these facts are constantly conjoined.*

Having bound the constant conjunction of ideas, images and feelings by giving it a name, the meaning of this conjunction can begin to build up. This is similar to labelling as alpha function the process or processes necessary for experience to be used in thinking. Having given it a label, meaning can begin to accumulate through psychoanalytic experience. When the young child labels the constantly conjoined elements 'Daddy', then the concept begins to be filled with meaning, and, indeed, the emotional meaning can continue to accrue indefinitely.

The constant conjunction is itself an abstraction from the many elements available. Giving a name to the constant conjunction is itself a further step in abstraction. The word is the name of the statement that the elements constantly occur together. If a man regularly feels angry when he sees his girlfriend happily engaged with a group of young men, it may help him to label it as 'the angry feeling I get when she is with others'. Giving the experience a name holds it together. Then the ramifications of its meaning for him can begin to accrete.

We now return to the coherence, the named abstraction which arose out of the PS↔D move. This is a thought and is capable of growth. To achieve this it has to be capable of acting as a pre-conception, that is, open to the realization which will fulfil it. It then becomes a conception. This has the effect of binding it and thus keeping it from dispersal. In this way the new thought is thus consolidated. It can then become unsaturated and available for further development.

Every emotional experience can be matched with an abstraction and with a theory (scientific deductive system) even if these have not yet been discovered. It may be possible to represent a new emotional experience by a scientific deductive system which has been derived from a prior emotional experience. It may be possible at some point, as in scientific hypotheses, to represent these in an algebraic equation or calculus; this is a further abstraction.

The greater the degree of abstraction, the more it can be generalized and the greater number of analytic situations it can apply to. A particular abstraction may then be found to fit a current psychoanalytic theory. For example, in the material of Mrs A in the previous chapter, her greater capacity for tolerating not-knowing and separation related to increased inner strength, and on abstraction this is seen to be the same as Melanie Klein's theory of relating inner psychic strength to introjection of the good object. Abstraction thus prevents the proliferation of so-called 'new' theories, which often, after sufficient distillation by abstraction, turn out to be examples of old, well-tried theories.

The abstraction may be too abstract to find a realization with which to mate, so it is necessary that the abstraction can be rendered more concrete, by moving back up the Grid towards row C; in practice, the abstraction can be described in terms of a model (see Chapter 9), and this includes myths (see Chapter 5). While resorting to a model may make the matter clearer and more vivid, it may, at the same time, render it less precise. The alternative is the more abstract representation which is more accurate but less comprehensible.

As mentioned above, the derived psychoanalytic object (the psychoanalytic object itself being unknowable) is comprised of a constant and a variable or unsaturated element, ψ (ξ), the saturation of which will then determine the value of the constant.

To summarize, in the process of the analytic session the analyst becomes aware of a previously unrecognized conjunction of elements in the patient's material. The recognition of this, arising out of the same material at which he has been gazing for some time, may be a startling experience, as when one suddenly sees the reversed perspective of a picture. When this is recognized and labelled, its meaning for the patient begins to grow, and, with this, the value of the particular manifestation of the psychoanalytic object. The K link or the getting-to-know function of the analyst abstracts from the manifestation of the psychoanalytic object something which can act as a pre-conception, which is different from an inborn pre-conception in that it already has a penumbra of meanings. It is therefore more restricted in the values with which it can be saturated. The inborn pre-conception is not so restricted.

THOUGHT AS THE LACK OF WISHED-FOR SATISFACTION

We have been describing thinking or the development of thoughts. Bion found it useful to postulate that there are thoughts without a thinker, that is, thoughts 'waiting' for a thinker to think them. This not only enables one to look at thoughts separately from the thinking process but gives an insight into how minute is the 'spectrum of sensuous existence' (Bion 1991: 160). But, as mentioned before (see Chapter 8), he also made a place for the development of thoughts within the personality. For this he put forward a model, that of a baby waiting for the breast which does not come. The baby is frustrated because his need for the breast is not being met. The very absence of the breast is experienced as the presence of something unpleasant; that is, the no-breast is a presence which is felt to be depriving the infant of what he wants, therefore it is felt to be a cruel, bad breast. Although we have called this a presence it is not, of course, sensuously present. This lack of wished-for sensory satisfaction is itself a thought. The no-thing is a thought. As Bion puts it, 'If there is no "thing", is "no thing" a thought and is it by virtue of the fact that there is "no thing" that one recognizes that "it" must be thought?' (Bion 1962: 35). In this case, it is the failure of an expectation which has led to a thought and therefore potentially to mental development. Thinking could lead for example, to the recognition that the good, satisfying breast is actually absent; that it has not changed after all into something cold, ungiving and malevolent, which is what happens when it is not thought about.

Alternatively, the unpleasant no-breast might not be tolerated in the mind long enough to become a thought; instead it might be treated as a thing to be got rid of, a foreign body to be expelled. If it is not thought, that is, if one does not actively think about this feeling experience, one is left with a bad figure who then *acts*. Clinically we see that those who have suffered severe infantile traumata frequently act in malevolent and psychopathic ways: action is the alternative pathway to that of thought. Similarly clinging to one's paranoid feelings or to self-punishment are aspects of not thinking the thought, the no-breast. These are also *actions*.

If evacuation of the painful experience takes place, blockage in mental development occurs. It is not a process confined to the severely disabled but something that we can observe in ourselves on a day-to-day or moment-to-moment basis. Rejection of painful feeling, refusal to think, blocks the development of thought. As a habit it results in a stultification of growth because it prevents the sort of thinking that could lead to growth. Thinking about the self remains stuck in a vicious circle.

REVERSIBLE PERSPECTIVE

Bion (1962b: 50–60) discusses another mode by which the patient avoids pain, which he calls *reversible perspective*. In this case the interpretation is accepted by the patient but the background assumption is altered. For instance the assumption that the analyst is the analyst may be silently denied. This alteration in perspective then prevents the interpretation from instituting change; it keeps the situation static. Just as with a picture which has a reversible perspective, it is not possible to detect whether someone sees the picture as two faces or a vase, so in the session it is not possible to detect which perspective is being seen by the patient as there is no sensible phenomenon by which it can be noted. All that one is aware of is the agreement with the interpretation, but there is no change. The question then is how is an analyst to note this reversible perspective? Bion's answer is to use the Grid to categorize the nature of the patient's response to the interpretation. Where the interpretation is F5 or F6 or G5 or G6, the patient's response is F1 or F2, that is, the interpretation which is designed to probe and institute change is dealt with merely as a definitory hypothesis, a statement of the analyst's views and of no relevance to the patient, or else it is used to block the truth. In fact the patient cannot always muster the necessary nimbleness of mind to reverse the perspective and then resorts to delusion or hallucination. When the analyst notices these more crude defences he may then be led to suspect the operation of reversible perspective at other times. Bion says that reversible perspective is evidence of pain. In a public lecture once at the Tavistock he said that the patient experiencing the psychoanalytic process says, 'It hurts.' The sense was that analysts tend to forget this.

Whereas the non-psychotic person, through alpha function, has potentially available an endless stream of images, in which every sensory modality is represented, on which to draw for the models and abstractions of thinking, the psychotic personality, because of disturbance in or reversal of alpha function, has no such source. Instead of being able to use his own internally produced images to represent the emotional situation which he needs to understand and to express, he has to use an external object.

Bion observed a patient who used external objects as signs to stand for his thoughts. This could be seen as a stage between thinking about concepts by manipulation of the objects themselves and thinking about objects in their absence. If the furniture in the consulting-room stands for his thoughts, then a change in the arrangement of the furniture may suddenly assume great significance to such a person because it is equated with a change in his mind.

A sensory impression might be taken in and stored unchanged until it can be used in the attempt to think. Bion describes a psychotic patient who remembered an occasion when Bion was wearing sunglasses. This image was stored, to be reproduced months and years later as a vehicle for representing many complex ideas, much as a Chinese character or ideograph can stand for many things (Bion 1967a: 56–8). This process differs from the normal process of storing images to be used later for thoughts in that in the latter, continual change is occurring in these images; they are allowed to interact, blend and fuse with others. The image of the sunglasses was not only unchanging but it was felt to be the thoughts themselves; it did not merely stand for these thoughts. Because of hatred of psychic reality, the sunglasses are turned into a thought by abolishing any emotional quality associated with them.

A young man, apparently very dependent on his analyst but unable to express his thoughts in any coherent way, was faced with the birth of his first child. At this time, he missed two sessions, even though he had found himself psychologically unable to get to the hospital in time for the baby's birth. At his next session, a striking change was noticeable in that, for the first time, he was able to express himself articulately. It seemed that the new baby and its needs enabled him to speak to his analyst in such a way that his analyst could comprehend the patient's own self. The concrete event of the baby's birth and early days acted for this man in a somewhat analogous way to that of the 'furniture' for Bion's patient: as concrete things standing for his own thoughts, which he could then manipulate in such a way as to begin to express something of his own emotional experience.

These examples, in which there is reliance on a suitable external object or occurrence to think with, represent varying stages between needing to manipulate concrete objects in order to think and being able to think about and manipulate objects in their absence.

An analyst being bombarded with intolerable material, meaningless material, believes that by going on waiting, watching and thinking meaning will eventually dawn. Meanwhile the patient who can't wait has to try to make sense of the material, perhaps by using some sort of theory. This putting together has no real ring of truth, but is the patient's attempt to do something with the intolerable material that has no $♀$ around because it has not yet registered that it is waiting in the analyst to be processed. This forcing of elements together is the agglomeration of beta elements to form a type of $♂$ or a net-like $♀$. This is similar to but not the same as PS↔D because the beta elements are not suitable to represent thoughts, therefore their agglomeration as opposed to coherence does not result in the 'spontaneous bleakness' of the truth.

Chapter 11

Transformations

There is an inherent truth which must be disengaged from the outward appearance of the object to be represented. This is the only truth that matters.

(Henri Matisse, quoted in Read 1974: 44)

I witness an event which moves me. I want to describe it to someone else. I put my experience into words, or, if I have some talent, I may paint the experience or express it in a poem. These are transformations of the original emotionally meaningful event. The essence of the original experience is still recognizable in the new form, provided that the recipient has sufficient understanding, experience and motivation.

In painting, a visual and emotional experience has to be rendered on a two-dimensional surface. How is this done? We know various rules are involved, such as those of perspective and colour to render the difference between near and far objects. A distant tree may be represented by blobs of different greens and blues. If it is painted with trunk and branches as the artist's mind might tell him to do, it no longer conveys the essence of the original situation. Something like prior knowledge has imposed itself and interfered with the accurate rendering of the original experience. Thus an artificial blinding to what one knows, is necessary to convey the original experience with some accuracy. This new version of the original experience is a transformation. In poetry, too, there are various rules of versification for the transformation of the original ineffable experience into the poem, rules relating to meaning and musical sense of the words, rhythm and scansion.

The analytic experience, the coming together of two personalities, cannot be known in its essence but only in its manifestations in the two people involved – analyst and patient. Each of them experiences it in his own unique way, represents it to himself, this being the first transformation, and then transforms it in and for communicating to the other just as does the artist or poet. It is then possible for the two versions of the same situation, that is, the transformation of the patient and that of the analyst, to be compared with each other. The patient's transformation is expressed in his behaviour both verbal and non-verbal; the analyst attempts to restrict his transformation to words, the interpretation. As with the artist, so with the analyst; his pre-conceptions may blind him to experiencing and being able to transform adequately his experience.

The primary but unknowable reality called O is represented by being transformed or processed in someone's mind. The process of transformation, *T alpha*, results in *T beta*, the product which can be observed by an other. T beta might be a painting, a scientific formula, a statement of a patient, an interpretation. There could be many different transformations of the same O. The analyst at the commencement of a session is faced with O, with which he tries to get in touch by free-floating attention and by keeping his mind artificially blinded to his expectations so as to leave himself as open as possible to this new experience. In Bion's terms, he keeps his mind, his pre-conceptions, as unsaturated with premature meaning as possible, so as to be receptive to the selected fact. This in turn is bound by a name and, with further time, will gradually accrue meaning from the events in the session.

These transformations – poetic, artistic, scientific, psychoanalytic – are all constructions of the mind expressed in particular ways. In mathematical transformations, formulae, geometrical drawings and graphs are signs for the relationships which mathematics is about; they are not the 'things-in-themselves'. They are transformations of the O of mathematics. Progressive cycles of transformations occur. A straight line on a graph can be transformed into an algebraic equation such as $x - 2y = 0$. This is a transformation from a visual image expressed in relation to two-dimensional space to an abstract representation which is more flexible but lacks the visual impact and sensual reality of the geometrical figure.

Of like nature to psychoanalytic transformations are those of geometry, particularly projective and algebraic geometry. Bion makes frequent use of constructions from these fields and a number of his terms such as invariant, vertex, point and line, projective transformation and others are taken directly from this branch of mathematics. Geometry concerns itself with logical relationships existing among given assumptions. Psychoanalysis concerns itself with the relationship between objects.

Projective geometry, as its name implies, is the geometry of point, line and space projected onto a field from a particular vertex; thus a geometrical figure is projected onto a surface or plane which may or may not be parallel to that of the original figure. (The artist's painting is a projection onto a flat surface of the three-dimensional subject he or she wishes to paint.) Certain relationships or properties remain the same under a projection. For example, in the original figure, two points A and B separate two other points C and D. This statement remains the same for the projected figure, even though the respective positions of C and D have changed. Such a property is said to be *invariant* under projection.

If the figure is projected onto a successive series of planes, certain features of the object remain unchanged. These are the invariants in the projection.

In order to express adequately the original essentially unknowable reality O, the transformations must contain these invariants or elements which are unchanged in the process of transformation, that is, there must be certain basic features which enable us to recognize the transformation as a representation of the original situation, for example recognizing that on the two-dimensional surface of the painting parallel lines are represented by two lines which converge on a point at the horizon. The invariant is the unchanging element in the psychoanalytic object, previously referred to as ψ, together with its unsaturated part, ξ.

To demonstrate invariants in an analytic situation, Bion gives a vivid illustration of a transformation by comparing the state of the analysis before and after a breakdown, that is, a situation contained in the analytic session compared with when it is uncontained and spilling out into others in the external world. In the pre-catastrophic stage, the analysis is

unemotional, theoretical, and devoid of any marked outward change. Hypochondriacal symptoms are prominent. The material lends itself to interpretations based on Kleinian theories of projective identification and internal and external objects.

Violence is confined to phenomena experienced by psycho
analytical insight; it is, as it were, theoretical violence.

By contrast, in the post-catastrophic stage the

> violence is patent ... emotion is obvious and aroused in the
> analyst. Hypochondriacal elements are less obtrusive. ...
> In this situation the analyst must search the material for
> invariants to the pre- and post-catastrophic stages ... certain
> apparently external emotionally-charged events are in fact the
> same events as those which appeared in the pre-catastrophic
> stage under the names, bestowed by the patient, of pains in the
> knee, legs, abdomen, ears, etc., and, by the analyst, of internal
> objects. In brief, what present themselves to the outward sense
> of analyst and patient as anxious relatives, impending law-suits,
> mental hospitals, certification and other contingencies appar-
> ently appropriate to the change in circumstances, are really
> hypochondriacal pains and other evidences of internal objects
> in a guise appropriate to their new status as external objects.
> These then are the invariants or objects in which invariance is
> to be detected.
>
> (Bion 1965: 8–9)

Post-catastrophe, an analyst in the United States started
sleeping with her patients. Pre-catastrophe she had been a much
admired analyst. In the post-catastrophic situation many
colleagues were shocked. In the pre-catastrophic situation several
analysts were shocked at her idealization of analysts and deni-
gration of therapists. The invariant therefore was to be looked
for in the shock waves that emanated from her both before and
after. The internal relationship is best portrayed by Munch's *The
Scream*.

Having named this process transformation, Bion proceeds to
investigate its meaning and usefulness in the armamentarium of
the analyst. He believes that a theory of transformations will aid
analytic observation, that the recognition and therefore binding
and naming of certain types of transformation will not only enable
a fuller understanding of the meaning to be reached but might
also aid in communicating with other analysts who have differing
theoretical backgrounds, by the recognition of the invariants in
the analytic situation.

Just as with the painter, if we can understand something about
the process of representation in the analytic transformation, we

can begin to delineate particular types of transformation which might then shed light on similar problems in other patients. To aid the recognition of the process of representation, the emphasis is not on the content of the communication but rather on the stage of development of the thought expressed and the use to which it is being put at that moment, that is, an attempt is made to place the particular statement, the T beta of the patient, into one of the Grid categories.

Bion gives an example in which the patient and analyst shake hands at the beginning of a session. From the patient's point of view, this gesture is a denial of his feelings of hostility towards the analyst. This would therefore be categorized as C2; C because of its descriptive quality, and column 2 because it is being used to mislead, that is, to deny his hostility. Subsequently it becomes apparent that the handshake of the analyst is experienced by the patient as a sexual assault. It is not a thought or fantasy about it but it is experienced as an actual sexual assault. The category is therefore row A, the beta elements, and it is in column 1 because it defines the relationship as the patient experiences it. The total transformation is therefore expressed as T = C2 to A1. It is possible that this pattern of transformation could be recognized in other patients and therefore be an aid in understanding.

The theory of transformations in its use of Grid categories enables the analyst to go on working on a problem in the absence of the patient. In this respect it is like mathematics; the actual objects do not have to be physically present to be thought about.

Growth or progress in thinking about a topic is represented in the Grid by progressive saturations of pre-conceptions giving rise to conceptions which in turn become the next pre-conceptions requiring saturation. This process can presumably continue indefinitely. It is represented on the Grid by movement down and across from left to right.

According to Freud, the desirable state of mind for the analyst is one of free-floating attention; in Grid terms D4 and E4. But as the analyst brings his theoretical knowledge and his experience to bear, his state of mind should be represented by a broader span, from rows C to F and columns 1, 3, 4 and 5. For example, once a constant conjunction has crystallized, it is named; this is a move from column 1 to column 3. At this point it becomes a pre-conception, row D. Its meaning gradually accumulates; a move from column 4 through column 5 to 6, and simultaneously from row D to E and F. The ubiquitous Oedipus theory in its many variations, including its part-object manifestations, can also be classified on the Grid as it makes its appearance in the material. Bion noted the following uses of the theory of transformations.

THE USE OF TRANSFORMATION THEORY IN DISTINGUISHING NEUROSIS FROM PSYCHOSIS

In the transference of classical psychoanalysis, the infantile object relationships are reproduced in the analytic situation and involve the person of the analyst or his representative in another. This transference occurs in a straightforward way without much distortion. The Oedipal relationship can usually be discerned without too much difficulty. This type of transformation is *rigid motion transformation* and is typical of the neurotic personality.

Using a geometrical way of thinking, we can look on this sort of transformation as similar to the projection of a photographic slide onto a parallel screen. The picture projected onto it is almost identical to the original slide. The figures and objects are not distorted and bear the same relation to each other as in the original. Thus with the rigid motion type of transformation the transferred relationships are more or less straightforward representations of the internal object relationships.

In contrast to this is the transformation typical of the psychotic part of the personality, which, owing to the considerable employment of the mechanisms of splitting and projective identification, is characterized by much confusion between patient and analyst. An impression of fragmentation and scattering is given, which is not necessarily confined to the personality of the analyst nor to the situation between analyst and patient. Rather the model may be one of an explosion into outer space, giving rise to a much more bizarre picture and hence much more difficult to observe and understand. This is *projective transformation*. The psychotic patient cannot tolerate thoughts because of their frustrating quality; the thought is a no-thing and frustration is inherent in its very nature. His alpha function is destroyed and therefore he has no visual images or conception of a three-dimensional space; hence his projections are felt to explode into boundless space, without co-ordinates to act as guidelines.

In this type of transformation, our photographic slide is now projected by the light source, at best onto a surface at an angle to the slide, or, at worst, out into space. The projected picture is distorted in a number of different ways yet certain features remain invariant.

In a projective transformation the patient may attribute to the analyst's personality something that occurred at a considerable distance and entirely unrelated to him. This is of course a surprise to the analyst and may not be recognized by him, leading to the situation in which the patient thinks that the analyst is mad because he appears not to know what his own actions are.

In his book *Further Learning from the Patient* Casement (1990: 79) gives an example of a rigid motion transformation. The patient's father died while he was at school, so, says Casement, absence became associated with death, and he says: 'In the transference illusion, I had become (between sessions) the dead father.'

Another patient complained that his wife was in a foul mood on a Friday evening. This was rage at the analyst's absence but it had been disowned in himself and projected into his wife. In another example the patient hallucinated fragmented images onto the walls of the consulting-room. This was a projective transformation of envious hatred of the analyst.

HYPERBOLE

Bion observed a common state of mind in which there are very strong emotions but these are powerfully projected out. He labelled this 'hyperbole'. The etymological roots of hyperbole are from the Greek words meaning 'over-throw, excess'. In geometry the arms of the hyperbola project to infinity, thus ideas associated with hyperbole are those of throwing to an immense distance as well as exaggeration. The powerful emotions may be of any sort, but basically idealizing or denigrating. The appearance of hyperbole in an analytic session is an indicator that *a transformation associated with rivalry, envy and evacuative projection* is taking place. This can take place with any link, L, H, or K, and may well involve acting out, hatred, love or megalomania. The emotion is exaggerated to draw attention to the self, and to get through to the object. If the object is impervious and rejecting, the exaggerated attempts to get through to the object are met with equally violent rejection. This, in turn, increases the force of the expressed emotions and so on in an escalating manner.

ANTI-GROWTH

As has been emphasized, mental growth is represented on the Grid by movement from left to right and down the vertical axis. We now look at that part of the self that is against development and is devoted to greedily and enviously devouring any and all aspects of existence, annihilating every meaningful object and occurrence. It is depicted as ↙↑, which stands for the negative of the two axes of the Grid. The anti-growth aspect is conveyed by the upward pointing arrow, representing a backward movement in the vertical or genetic axis of the Grid from developing sophisticated meaning towards the meaningless beta elements. The arrow pointing to the left does not mean from columns 6 and 5 towards column 1 but rather the negative of that horizontal axis in the sense of column 2; thus all the uses to which a thought may be put as represented by columns 1, 3, 4, 5 and 6 are now used for the purpose of preventing the emergence of something true. The negative Grid is thus an elaborated version of the column 2 category, minus versions of categories in columns 1, 3, 4, 5, 6 and any columns that might be added to the Grid in the future $(n - 1)$. A statement categorized as minus column 4, for example, would have the function of drawing attention to something for the purpose of negating a potentially growth-promoting state, that is, denying access to the emergence of truth.

This negative Grid is the domain of –K. Bion believes that stupor has the same configuration as this violent, greedily ambitious part. He relates this to the frightening quality of the infinite space associated with –K, that is, of the explosive projection into 'an immensity so great that it cannot be represented even by astronomical space because it cannot be represented at all' (Bion 1970: 12). In stupor there is extreme opposition to any movement or liveliness, but there is commonly periodic violence. He labels this ↙↑. This sign is used so that its meaning can remain open to a certain extent and not be swamped by other associations to the words 'greed', 'envy', 'ambition' and so on.

An example of the change to –K can be seen when a patient's appreciation of an interpretation is followed immediately by associations which indicate that what he now feels he has been given is something nasty, insulting and deliberately wounding. The meaningfulness of the interpretation has been removed. Sometimes an interpretation is seen to pass into both positive and negative networks at once, giving rise to both appreciation and contemptuous rejection.

Another example[1] of retreat into –K is that of the patient who developed an attack of sneezing and an itching throat, that is, hay-fever, immediately following a painful insight, a reversal turning the meaningful experience into beta elements, which were then evacuated.

When $\leftarrow\uparrow$ is dominant, the patient's fear is that she has rendered everything meaningless by greedily attacking and destroying meaning. Hence her use of analysis is determined by a need to get the analyst to speak, the interpretations being a proof to the patient that there is, after all, meaning in her own words and life. The interpretation is taken only as a reassurance and not for its growth-promoting potential. If the analyst does not realize this, an analytic impasse can result in the sense of a parasitic type of relationship, the patient wanting only reassurance, which by its very nature has to be constantly repeated. Therefore no mental development takes place.

Certain of these patients give a waif-like impression of living from hand to mouth. Their fear of the meaninglessness of life is masked by their apparent satisfaction with their way of life, which complacency seems unfounded in view of its apparent time-wasting pointlessness. Addiction is often a feature, as is their addiction to analysis. Repeated attempts are made, often with extreme subtlety, to provoke critical comments from the analyst. Any silent reflection on the analyst's part is taken by the patient as disapproval. When the analyst speaks, however, there is an immediate change in the patient to excited pleasure and talka-tiveness. When the use of the analysis as a reassurance against the fear that his life was meaningless was interpreted to one patient, he responded with understanding, saying that it was the same with music; when listening to a particular type of music, he felt powerful, that he could achieve anything he desired, but when the music ceased he was again in an unmotivated state. Music was proof that meaning and life had not, after all, been destroyed.

Truth is growth-promoting and anti-truth psychically debili-tating. The psychotic or the psychotic part of the personality does not accept this dictum, in fact it promotes the opposite point of

---

[1] See also the example of the reversal of alpha function in Chapter 7

view, that lies are nourishing and truth destructive. This can be clearly seen in action in *transformations in hallucinosis*.

TRANSFORMATION IN HALLUCINOSIS

This particular form of transformation reveals the inadequacy of our usual analytic methods of observation and notation. By recognizing this particular transformation, the analyst is able to re-orientate himself in the patient's material and not get caught in a particular trap. In this transformation the patient is rivalrous with the analyst, believing that his mode of so-called self cure is superior to analysis. Thus he believes that the analyst, in carrying out his analytic function, is competitively trying to prove that his method is superior to that of his patient. If, however, he does not analyse, then the patient assumes triumphantly that his own technique is superior to that of the analyst. This Catch 22 situation can be avoided when it is seen as a transformation in hallucinosis.

This is also a transformation by the psychotic part of the personality with its hatred of psychic reality. Intolerance of frustration results in the mind being used as a muscular organ of expulsion like the rectum or bladder. It must therefore be understood in the session that the significance of the patient's speech might be only that he is getting rid of something he does not want by expelling it in the spoken word. He is getting rid of the meaningful experience by expulsion as if it were a thing not a thought. To the experienced listener the words may convey a flavour of the experience which is being expelled. The Grid category to focus on is A6, the expulsion of beta elements, thoughts that are felt to be the actual things themselves.

The patient believes that he is independent of the analyst, that he can be the perfect object to himself, being able to produce whatever is necessary for his survival at any moment when a need is felt. Thus frustration, envy and other anxieties are obliterated and there is a ready solution to the ever-present greed. Whatever is desired can be produced by hallucinatory methods.

This occurs as follows. The sensory organs function in reverse; instead of their normal function of taking in sensory data, the sense organs, in whatever sensory modality is favoured, excrete, as it were, images into the external world. These hallucinated images are then 'perceived', seen, heard, smelt, felt, as if real, and provide instant satisfaction to the omnipotent self. The emotional experience, the reality of the session, is transformed into sense impressions, which are then evacuated as hallucinations, yielding pleasure or pain but not meaning. The latter can only arise through tolerating frustration long enough for recognition and naming – 'even if the name is no more than a grunt or yell' (Bion 1970: 10) for a constant conjunction to occur, following which meaning begins to accrue.

Analysis tends to disturb this process by casting doubt on whether hallucinatory satisfaction is as satisfying as reality. There is a lessening of omnipotence and a feeling that the ability for instant gratification has been lost. It is assumed therefore that the analyst has stolen or destroyed this ability, the analyst's motive undoubtedly being rivalry with the patient's supposed superior methods of 'cure'. The only relationship in transformations in hallucinosis is one of superior to inferior.

This situation, whereby analyst and patient are felt to be promulgating rival methods of treatment, makes for a particular difficulty in analysis. By making interpretations that have the effect of lessening the patient's ability to profit by hallucinosis, the analyst is felt thereby to be competing rivalrously with the patient, as though determined to prove the superiority of his psychoanalytic method. If he does not interpret, however, then he is assumed to have conceded defeat to his superior rival. The whole situation of this false polarization therefore needs to be addressed in the interpretation so that the patient is not left with a belief in the analyst's rivalry with him.

THE DOMAIN OF THOUGHT

The state of nothing cannot be imagined but it can be thought or expressed in mathematical symbols. If it were said that beyond the universe there is nothing, we can imagine a sort of boundary fence at the end of the universe and we cannot stop ourselves imagining what it would be like to look out over the fence; it is not possible to imagine nothing. We therefore think of psycho-analysis in visual terms of internal objects in a mental three-dimensional space, into which we project parts of ourselves. This restricts our thinking in the way that mathematics was restricted when it was represented totally by geometry. We need to be able to represent the mental domain in a more abstract or algebraic way so that it can retain the potential for development, represented by the unsaturated part of ψ (ξ). This would also open up the possibility of deriving a formulation sufficiently generalized to cover a great range of eventualities. Mental space cannot be known but it can be represented, for example by points and lines.

Bion postulates that geometry arose out of emotional experience, that it developed as a way of trying to express the place or space where a feeling or object was. He uses the point and line in various ways. The point is used to represent the place where the object or emotion was. If the absence of the object cannot be tolerated and therefore thought about, the point comes to represent a 'no-thing', a frightening ghost, a damaged, diminished breast. The space where a thought might arise is already filled; it is saturated, therefore there can be no thought and no development. The point thus represents also the place where something could be. In this way it can represent a pre-conception available to join with a realization to form a conception and thus promote mental growth. The point as a pre-conception pertains to the vertical axis of the Grid.

We can conceive the domain of thought as being composed of no-things waiting to become thoughts, and potential constant conjunctions waiting to be observed. Where the object no longer is becomes the emotional experience which can be transformed into something meaningful if the associated frustration and pain can be tolerated. Tolerance of the frustration arising from experience of the no-object can lead to a thought or recognition of a constant conjunction or pattern, following which an appropriate realization that matches it can be looked for. The realization enables the pre-conception to be made into a conception and to undergo further development in meaning. When frustration and pain cannot be tolerated, the no-thing is felt to be a thing to be got rid of, so no constant conjunction can be noted. The imperfection of any realization which mates with a pre-conception also gives rise to frustration which, if not tolerated, will prevent matching. In the psychotic the matching has to be extremely close for mating to occur. Hence the pre-conception often remains unsaturated or else mates up with a wrong realization which results in a misconception or delusion.

Patients can saturate elements in the analysis using words in such a way that their meaning has been destroyed; they mark the place where the meaning used to be. Effectively they have become beta elements. Hence one may listen to a description of day-to-day events without any thoughts, ideas, feelings or meaning being evoked. This represents a failure to transform the reality of the session, O, a blockage of the space or point where something could arise. The space becomes a dead-space, no life-giving interchange can take place. Psychotic patients fear unsaturated words because they equate them with greed, from the projection and fragmentation of the enviously greedy aspect ↲↑ seeking to swallow any existence it comes across. They therefore want to keep words saturated with stale meaning. This may manifest itself clinically by a monotonous description of events.

Using the idea that geometry developed to express emotional meaning, Bion sees the line as representing the place to which the point may be going, which is another way of saying the use to which the thought may be put, that is, it relates to the horizontal axis of the Grid. Again the line bears the significance of the place where the penis was and also where something could be in the future. For growth to occur, these two concepts have to be brought together.

What Bion is looking for is an accurate way of describing the invariants of the transformations taking place in the analytic session, so that their essence can be seen. Point and line, the place where something was and the place where something could arise, breast and penis, the two axes of the Grid, are all ways of expressing the relationship which is the invariant in the transformation. This invariant is what is in common between the ellipse in the painting and the round pond it represents, the drawing of the railway lines to meet at a point and the reality of parallel rail tracks. 'If there is a "no-thing" the "thing" must exist ... the invariant under psychoanalysis is the ratio of no-thing to thing' (Bion 1965: 103). For example, in claustrophobia and agoraphobia, there is a common denominator or invariant although the initial clinical presentation may be very different. The space, either inside the object as in claustrophobia or outside the object as in agoraphobia, is intolerable. This space represents emotions indistinguishable from the 'place where something was', that is, in these patients who cannot tolerate the absence of the object there is a present non-existent object which renders the 'space' frightening, whether experienced as inside or outside the object. Panic is being trapped in this space with no means of escape, that is, there can be no thought by which escape could be effected. This is the invariant in both claustrophobia and agoraphobia and this is also the space represented by geometrical space. A geometrical figure may then be seen as representing relationships between objects; the claustrophobic situation can be represented by a point within a circle, the agoraphobic by a point outside a circle and not touching it. Understanding the invariants obviates the need for both terms, agoraphobia and claustrophobia; they are different manifestations of the same problem.

Transformations are the ways in which the patient attempts to solve his problem. His particular transformations are unsuccessful. In the analytic relationship he has the opportunity of comparing his transformations of a particular situation with those of the analyst.

The analyst can decide on any one of a number of choices for his transformation of his experience with the patient. There is no one correct interpretation but the analyst's choice both arises out of and commits him to his relationship with the patient, the O. The analyst's statements hopefully are restricted to the K link; they should not include either H or L links and they are in Grid categories of F1, 3, 4, 5. These concepts that form the analyst's interpretation arise from his understanding, that is, his pre-conception, which has met with a realization arising from something external to himself, that is, arising from his relationship with his patient.

The patient's statements, however, can be linked by any of L, H or K links, including –K (which can be taken to include –L and –H), and they can be classifiable under any Grid category. Similarly he can take the analyst's interpretation in any way he chooses, for example as an instrument for self-flagellation, as a confirmation of fusion, as evidence that the analyst has stolen his ideas from him and so on.

TRANSFORMATIONS IN –K

There is a hatred and fear of transformations in K because they may result in closer approximations to becoming O, or at-one-ment with O. An interpretation may be accepted in K, that is, knowing about it, but rejected in O, becoming it. The patient comes to the session but institutes –K activity in a projective transformation which is category A6. Hyperbole is in operation. So we now look again at ↙↑ and transformations in –K to see in what ways it might be possible to work with this in a session, that is, to try to see the meaning in the –K link of depletion of meaning. ↙↑ could be thought of as a non-existent 'it' whose aim is to suck the existence out of any object or situation which it encounters.

How does a transformation in –K manifest itself clinically? We are dealing with a projective transformation into multidimensional 'space'. The area of projection is not confined to the delimited area of rigid motion transformation which is usually onto the analyst or his representative. Instead it is multidimensional and therefore cannot be understood by us in visual terms. The projection can be in part into the analyst, into a variety of external objects, and out into space, that is, unlimited multidimensional mental space. There are vague references to a variety of subjects and objects, some of which may be hallucinations. This is the –K space and it is filled with no-objects, envious of and greedy for objects that have existence. Categorization on the Grid of the patient's statements allows the element of thought to remain unsaturated with meaning so that it is free to accumulate the gradually emerging meaning of –K activity for a particular patient.

VERTEX

One of the invariants in psychoanalysis is that of awareness or consciousness. This quality of awareness or consciousness is like the vertex of projective geometry from which the observed figure is viewed. Thus it is a point of view. There are unlimited possible vertices – religious, aesthetic, scientific, financial, ocular, auditory, digestive, respiratory, reproductive and so on. This gives a flexibility and enables the object, that is, T beta (patient) and T beta (analyst), to be viewed from different perspectives much as someone with a camera might take many shots of a figure from many different angles to obtain a more complete representation of it. The results will reflect the type of vertex from which they were viewed.

The analyst may find a change of vertex helpful in giving a new perspective on what seems to be a stuck situation. In a sense this change of vertex always occurs when we suddenly 'see' the meaning of the patient's behaviour. For example, a raging bullying man who is about to throw in his job because he has, in his words, been 'treated like shit' is suddenly seen as a little boy having a tantrum because of his ungovernable fury at being left alone.

It is common to get caught up in a sado-masochistic relationship as a defence against change. A patient repeatedly told the analyst he was no good, that analysis was useless, and that he, the patient, would leave, but made no plans to do so. Material was withheld except for the above complaints and threats. Occasional complaints were made about his being cruelly treated in the outside world. The analyst was aware of being provoked into retaliatory anger or helplessness. When the cruel victimization of the analyst was recognized as a primitive sexuality and was therefore seen as this patient's way of relating to the analyst, the feeling of provocation vanished. This is an example of a change of perspective resulting in development.

Even beta elements which are not a part of thought can be viewed as having some sort of proto-consciousness. ↙↑ as a beta element is searching for existence. Bion prefers to call this searching a *tropism*, 'an awareness of a lack of existence that demands an existence', 'a psyche seeking for a physical habitation to give it existence, ♀ seeking ♂" (Bion 1965: 109). The latter means ♀ seeking something to contain to give it coherence, and therefore the possibility of accumulating meaning. It can therefore be associated with *intuition*, which can itself then be brought to realization. The relationships expressed in and by the constant conjunction are intuitive and later realized; the pattern is noted, and later accretes meaning. This reminds us of one of Bion's descriptions of a beta element as 'something which may exist; not a thought, but that might become what thinkers describe as a thought, e.g. if a dog comes when it is called' (Bion 1991: 589).

ULTIMATE REALITY AND TRANSFORMATION IN O

There is an ultimate reality which cannot be known but can only be 'become', that is, it is possible to be at one with it. It stands for the truth of any object. It 'is not good or evil; it cannot be known, loved, or hated' (Bion 1965: 139). We all consciously or unconsciously believe that it is better not to 'become' it, but rather to keep a barrier of some sort between ourselves and the truth. O is this ultimate reality, equated with the truth, and is approached by mental growth as represented by movement down the Grid.

Resistance in analysis or in the group is to the emergence of O, resistance to harbouring the new thought. Often in a scientific discussion, the gradual emergence of a mutual understanding between opposing sides is interrupted by a 'well-meant' statement, ostensibly intended to clarify further but which results instead in a falling back to the mutually opposed positions.

We cannot know O itself but only emanations from it which are perceived as phenomena. What we know of O are our transformations of it. O can only be known about. We can also be identified with O, but this is not the same as being O. But by coming into contact with something that we perceive of as beautiful or good, for example when we experience a moment of being profoundly struck by a truth, we are reminded of O, just as Plato believed we are reminded of the ultimate Ideas of Beauty and Goodness. In a slightly different way, transient experiences of becoming O can be felt as being 'allowed' to us by the object; this is the experience of being at one with O, no matter for how short a time. and is an experience like incarnation, becoming of the same flesh. This experience of being at one with O, being O, is to be clearly differentiated from a process of projective identification in which one becomes God. This is madness, megalomania.

As Bion (1965: 139) points out, these experiences only occur after submission to 'an exacting discipline of relationships'. The first discipline involves relinquishing dependence on the usual forms of assurance derived from the evidence of the senses; for example, from using the content of the patient's statements as concrete evidence of the correctness of one's interpretation. Reliance on this sort of evidence results in column 2 interpretations, a manifestation of resistance in the analyst to facing the inevitability of uncertainty, often of a profound degree in the analytic encounter. It is also necessary to give up memory and desire as these fill the mind's potential space with sensible phenomena.

Another discipline required is the 'act of faith' (F) in the need to eschew this sort of evidence so that one's mind may be kept open to 'receive' understanding of a true aspect of the current relationship. 'F reveals and makes possible experiences that are often painful and difficult for the individual analyst and analysand to tolerate' (Bion 1970: 46). A third discipline is that of overcoming a specific fear of the transformation from knowing about O to becoming O. This fear is of going mad in the sense of the megalomania by becoming 'God' rather than being at one with O; –K is involved in this transformation into becoming 'God' rather than O.

It is much easier to know about something rather than to become it. Learning about analysis is easy but learning through the living of that aspect of the self, that is, by being it, is not. We would much rather know about ourselves than be ourselves, especially those aspects of ourselves retrieved by analysis from obscurity, to which we relegated them. 'I just want to know the facts about myself, but nothing of this interactive process.'

Resistance to the truth is expressed by a retreat to column 2 phenomena; lies are preferable to the truth, turning a blind eye is preferable to focusing the eyes on a fact, speaking only about so-called 'relevant' facts is preferable to trying to comment on what one is aware of, including what one feels reluctant to bring into the open. Prolonged analysis with very little change results when regular resort to column 2 mechanisms becomes a habit of mind so 'that the state of being "O" is indefinitely postponed'(Bion 1965: 149). Hence the importance of detecting these column 2 statements. Of course it is usually not only the analyst who feels dissatisfied with the meagre results of the above column 2 phenomena. As Bion points out, there is no resistance unless there is also a contrary feeling that becoming conscious of something alien in oneself is the most useful approach.

Ultimate reality can be thought of as a vast reservoir of infinite possibilities, of thoughts awaiting a thinker, from the derivatives of which, the transformations, we cull from time to time elements that seem to belong together, that form a pattern or constant conjunction. These elements we bind together by a name or a number so that they become available to be filled with meaning, so that we come to understand the emotional significance for us of this particular bit of reality. This understanding can then join up with another constant conjunction to accrue further meaning and so on indefinitely.

CYCLES OF TRANSFORMATION

The O of the session, unknowable in itself, is expressed through the phenomena that represent it. The T alpha of the patient transforms this experience and the resulting transformation, T beta (patient), is what is expressed in the patient's statement.

The phenomena representing O of the session for the analyst are similarly transformed to produce T beta (analyst). The analyst's transformation should be through a K link, while the patient's may be in L, H, K or –K. There may be progressive cycles of transformation depending on what the analyst detects.

To illustrate this we use an example of Bion's. He takes the statement 'The sun will rise tomorrow.' This can be classified on the Grid, which will focus the analyst's attention on the kind of statement being made by the patient. If this untrue statement is made about the weather, it is not being used to mislead but rather for purposes of notation or of drawing attention, thus it acts as a pre-conception, therefore D3 or 4. If such a statement were made in analysis as a hopeful response to an interpretation, this would be a transformation in O. If, however, it is an idealized statement about going out with his girlfriend, then it is a descriptive exaggerated term used to convey information, C3. It is an example of hyperbole, with an L link, and it is an example of a rigid motion transformation: the qualities of the sun rising being projected onto his relationship with his girl. This could be taken as the analyst's first cycle of transformation. Later, however, the analyst may consider it to be a denial of the patient's feelings of hostility towards him. In this second cycle of the analyst's transformation, the link is H; hyperbole is still in evidence as the hostility is projected far away and denied, therefore it is column 2, C2. This is a projective transformation to rid himself of hostility.

We can look at the sort of object presenting in the patient's material: is it fragmented or whole, present or absent? Is the linkage in K (putting together) or in H (splitting asunder), or in –K (meaninglessness)? The statement can be categorized according to the Grid and assessed as to its position in the change from transformations in K to transformations in O. It is necessary to achieve this latter transformation to become real. Many patients complete an analysis without ever having an experience of personal enlightenment, of at-one-ment with O.

For example, a patient's statement 'How is it that I have been coming to analysis for so long but I still don't have any self-confidence?' was said with provocative annoyance so that the status quo of sadomasochism could be maintained. It was met with the analyst's response: 'But perhaps you *haven't* got anything from the analysis', as a statement of possible fact. It aroused shock and rage and this was the moment in which the patient became real to himself.

Chapter 12

The study of groups

The self-deception in virtue of which a human individual regards himself as real in his separateness from all things, and presupposes this fictitious isolation to be the true ground and only starting-point for all his relations – this self-deception of abstract subjectivism plays terrible havoc not only in the domain of metaphysics – which, indeed, it abolishes altogether – but also in the domain of the moral and political life.

(Solovyov 1918: 200)

Before his mature studies on the nature of the psychoanalytic process and thinking, Bion had already done pioneering work with groups. Throughout this work we can see foreshadowed many aspects of his later works. As we trace through his work on groups we shall try to show the threads that connect this work with his more mature ideas.

When Bion reached the age of 50, the Professional Committee of the Tavistock Clinic asked him to take therapeutic groups, using his own techniques. In response to this request, he wrote,

It was disconcerting to find that the Committee seemed to believe that patients could be cured in such groups as these. It made me think at the outset that their expectations of what happened in groups of which I was a member were very different from mine. Indeed, the only cure of which I could speak with certainty was related to a comparatively minor symptom of my own – a belief that groups might take kindly to my efforts.

(Bion 1961: 29)

He mentions that he had had the experience of trying to persuade groups of patients to make the study of their tensions a group task. This was what has become known as the Northfield experiment, which we shall consider below.

Bion set about studying groups through observation and interpretation. He therefore combined the observational and experimental method. Interpretations are interventions which alter the behaviour of the group, so he observed the effect of these interpretations. As the group was his object of study he did not interpret the behaviour of individuals, though he was tempted to do so. So the members of the group would take their places and expected him to say something, explain how they were to proceed or do something to set the ball rolling. Instead of fulfilling their expectations he interpreted their expectations, of him and discovered that these interventions were most unwelcome. Through such a procedure he observed the way the group functioned and formulated certain principles thereon.

A group has a consciously designated task. The co-operative mental activity that is engaged in this task Bion named the work group. The term *work group* refers not to the people who constitute the group but to the mental activity in which they are engaged. This is the group which tries to look at itself and the group process scientifically, to observe itself, and to contain and speak about feelings rather than discharge them. Bion observed, however, another level of mental activity. To focus on this level was like focusing on a different layer of a too-thick microscope slide; one focus revealed the work group, but a shift in mental focus revealed another level of mental activity in which the group appeared to take no responsibility for what was happening, for example the banal level of conversation, and they did not appear to be listening when Bion made an interpretation. This other level of mental activity Bion called *basic assumptions*.

> Work group activity is obstructed, diverted, and on occasion assisted, by certain other mental activities that have in common the attributes of powerful emotional drives. These activities, at first sight chaotic, are given a certain cohesion if it is assumed that they spring from basic assumptions common to all the group.
>
> (Bion 1961: 146)

In a group there is always a basic assumption active at any one moment in time. There are three basic assumptions and if one is present then the other two are thereby excluded. The basic assumptions are the dependent group, the fight–flight group and the pairing group, and like the work group each of these describes a mode of mental functioning of the group, not the persons who constitute it.

In the dependent group one person is selected and then expected to fulfil the role of provider to other members of the group, or, as Bion puts it:

> The basic assumption in this group culture seems to be that an external object exists whose function it is to provide security for the immature organism. This means that one person is always felt to be in a position to supply the needs of the group, and the rest in a position in which these needs are supplied.
>
> (Bion 1961: 74)

The selected person relieves the rest from the need to be responsible, to think and work out things for themselves. In the therapeutic group the selected person is usually the psychiatrist, psychologist or psychoanalyst. When the analyst interprets the way the group is functioning, his intervention is most unwelcome. The group believes it has a right to expect this appointed leader to behave in the way which it wants. When he does not behave according to expectations the group believes he is being perverse or deliberately provocative.

The dependent group culture is in each of us but only becomes observable when human beings are in visible and audible relation to one another. Bion disagrees with the view that an instinct – the herd instinct – comes into operation when people gather together in numbers but is absent when an individual is in isolation from the group. He says we are groupish beings and those elements are operative in us all the time but they only become observable when we are in a group: 'The apparent difference between group psychology and individual psychology is an illusion produced by the fact that the group brings into prominence phenomena that appear alien to an observer unaccustomed to using the group' (Bion 1968: 134).

Our individual psychic make-up is intimately related to others, both the tendency to form constructively working groups and the potential, or valency, as Bion called it, for forming any of the basic assumption mental states when in a physical group setting with others.

Bion says that the basic assumption of the group is that 'people come together as a group for the purposes of preserving the group'

(Bion 1968: 63). That the grouping tendency is made manifest in the act of coming together is clear, but to postulate that the basic assumption of the individuals of the group is that they foregather to preserve the group suggests that they feel that the group has a natural tendency to disintegrate. This is what the group members fear and endlessly discuss when, for example, some member is absent. But there is no corresponding tendency of working to make the group worth preserving. Being in the group is, for a long time, felt to be all that is necessary.

In the groups it was made clear to Bion that although the assumption was that people had gathered in order to preserve the group, the object of this preservation was the group functioning under one of the basic assumptions. The group members' numerous complaints that they could not see what the interpretations, the emotions to which Bion was trying to draw their attention, had to do with their problems, that they could not remember what had happened in previous groups, indicated their difficulty in learning from experience. The process of development itself is hated. Bion, however, goes on to say:

> this is not simply a negative attitude; the process of development is really being compared with some other state ... like arriving fully equipped as an adult fitted by instinct to know without training or development exactly how to live and move and have his being in a group. There is only one kind of group that approximates to this dream, and that is ... the group dominated by one of the three basic assumptions.
>
> (Bion 1961: 89)

Bion understood that this antipathy to learning from experience was the major factor underlying all defensive stances. He entitled one of his books *Learning from Experience*, and his elaborations of this formed his life's work.

An individual can contribute anonymously to the group without having to take individual responsibility for this contribution. But there is a penalty for this; that person does not then receive recognition as an individual and the problems which brought him or her to the group will not be addressed as such. The basic assumption mentality ignores the individual, who is therefore in two minds about his or her group membership.

Another basic assumption of the group is the view that fighting and running away are the only mechanisms it can use to preserve the group. The idea of using understanding is anathema to the fight–flight group.

The key to understanding the fight–flight group is in the following sentence:

> There will be a feeling that the welfare of the individual does not matter so long as the group continues, and there will be a feeling that any method of dealing with neurosis that is neither fighting neurosis nor running away from the owner of it is either non-existent or directly opposed to the good of the group; a method like my own is not recognized as proper to either of the basic techniques of the group.
>
> (Bion 1961: 64)

The group looks for a leader who will lead the group either in flight from the enemy, that is, the feared state of mind, or to fight with the suffering victim; when the psychoanalyst or psychologist leader of the work group does not participate in this attitude, he is felt to be shirking. A more suitable leader is then found in someone who already has an enemy in mind, for example, someone who is paranoid. The group therefore may choose a leader who is frequently the most disturbed member of the group; if not overtly paranoid, then possibly someone with psychopathic tendencies. The enemy .as perceived by the group is the work group state of mind and what it threatens in the way of insight and painful feelings.

Bion's method, which is the work group mentality, is inimical to the basic techniques of the group because he continues to pursue clarification of that psychopathology which the group would prefer to flee from or else obliterate. Paradoxically Bion's method is caring of the individual through making a stand for observation and thinking which will then lead to mental development. He will not collude with the group's desire to locate an 'enemy' perhaps in an individual or even in an idea. Instead he interprets the group's desire to do just this. Just as in the dependent group one person is selected as the provider to the group; in the fight–flight group an enemy is selected and, either through fight or flight in relation to this enemy, the group 'feels' cohesive. In reality, however, the group has not solved its underlying disintegration but merely and temporarily hidden from itself this knowledge. Through the mechanism of fight or flight the group tries to destroy knowledge through action. Bion was able to achieve knowledge through containing the anxieties that were forced upon him in the group.

Sometimes in a group two people would start an interchange with each other and this was tolerated by the other members. This change of mood in the group was defined by Bion as the 'pairing group'. The group assumed, another basic assumption, that when two people meet together they do so for purposes of sex. Bion proposed that the other members of the group tolerated this exclusive exchange because sex gave rise to the hope that a child would be born in the future, what Bion termed a Messianic idea, that would have positive implications for the group in the sense of releasing them from their sense of bondage. The leader in the pairing group is therefore as yet unborn. The group's sense of bondage is the attitude of the work group which threatens them with the painful feelings of change.

It is the attitude of hopeful expectation to which the group clings in its anxious wish to get rid of the threat of having to learn from experience. There must be only hopeful expectation; the significant point is that the child of the pairing must never be born. A birth of a new idea, for example, would spell both loss of hope and change. Hence a new idea must be denied by statements such as 'This is not a new idea after all, it is just . . .'. In societal groups and institutions, this antipathy to the new idea is so ubiquitous as to pass almost unnoticed.

The differential focusing on the work group activity and on the present basic assumption reminds us of Bion's description of the psychic 'binocular vision' produced by the contact barrier of alpha elements which allows the simultaneous interweaving of unconscious and conscious elements, giving rise to depth and resonance in thinking and analytic intuition. This was later elaborated away from the dichotomy of unconsoious and conscious to the idea of viewing the psychoanalytic object from multiple vertices and also that of reversible perspective. In this way Bion moved psychoanalysis away from a positivistic stance.

In his re-view of group functioning, the last section of his book on groups, Bion, with his new understanding of Kleinian theory, postulated that the basic assumption group mentality was an attempt to obliterate persecutory feelings because

> the group approximates too closely, in the minds of the individuals composing it, to very primitive phantasies about the contents of the mother's body. The attempt to make a rational

investigation of the dynamics of the group is therefore perturbed by fears, and mechanisms for dealing with them, that are characteristic of the paranoid-schizoid position.

(Bion 1961: 162)

Bion later saw something similar in the psychotic's desperate attempts to prevent integration, even to the extent of destroying his mental apparatus. At the time of writing his papers on psychosis, Bion wrote about the psychotic's fear that integration would lead to the emergence of the terrifying savage super-ego. Later he was to speak instead of the catastrophic anxiety that occurs at moments of psychic change and that it is this that is so vigorously defended against by the attitude represented by the basic assumption mentality, which can also be seen as non-thinking and therefore associated with a –K or non-emotional link. In other words, his later formulation was that it was not just persecutory figures, and feelings, such as anxiety and guilt that were dreaded, but also the catastrophic loss of one's sense of security that is associated with mental change.

In trying to understand what lay behind the basic assumption group activity, Bion postulates figures from a fragmented primitive Oedipal myth. In the dependent group, there is one mature parent linked with one child, like Oedipus with his mother, as each group member tries to claim the leader for his or her own. In the fight–flight group one can see both the flight from the oracle's prediction and flight from the truth; the fight aspect being the killing of Laius, which stands for the obliteration of the necessary boundary between self and other, between individual and group. In the pairing group, there are two parents but the child, the future leader, has to remain unborn. What is not seen in any of the basic assumption mentalities is the coming together of two mature parents to produce a live and active child, which symbolically is the new and therefore threatening idea.

This foreshadows Bion's later work on mythology and his realization that it was not the narrative of these myths that was so important but rather the separate elements; that these elements could be recognized in an analytic session and shed illumination. Similarly he understood that it was not only the sexual elements of the Oedipus story that were important in psychic life, but that the elements of the story, as opposed to its narrative, were of cardinal importance in the structure of our thinking processes. For example, in this work on groups, the importance of the threatening sphinx figure is brought out.

> In so far as I am felt to be leader of work-group function, and recognition of that fact is seldom absent, I, and the work-group function with which I am identified, am invested with feelings that would be quite appropriate to the enigmatic, brooding, and questioning sphinx from whom disaster emanates. In fact terms are sometimes employed, on occasions when my intervention has provoked more than the usual anxiety, which hardly require interpretation to enable the group to grasp the similarity. I know of no experience that demonstrates more clearly than the group experience the dread with which a questioning attitude is regarded.
>
> (Bion 1961: 162)

The work group in its inquiry represents this. The group feels extremely threatened by this inquiry because of the fear of what will be revealed – damage, murder, incest, guilt, persecution, basically the devastating upheaval of the old order of things. The basic assumption group activity is against inquiry because it fears the pain of these emotional consequences.

The first chapter of *Experiences in Groups* is the reprint of an article which was published by Bion and John Rickman in *The Lancet* in 1943, in which they both describe the experiment in the military psychiatric hospital at Northfield, where the former had been put in charge of the training wing. Bion found that he could not get down to any serious planning there because he would be interrupted in his office by a series of importunate requests. He knew then that what was required was discipline and set himself the model of a commander in charge of a 'scallywag battalion'. Two elements were necessary: a common enemy and a commander who believed in the integrity of his men and was not afraid of either their admiration or their hostility. The enemy he designated as 'extravagant expressions of neurosis'.

We want to draw attention here to something that is central to Bion's self-understanding. When he found that he could not get down to any work because of constant interruptions which were of neurotic origin, he might well have issued an order that he was not to be interrupted between 10.00 a.m. and midday, but this was not his way. He drew the conclusion that the frustration he was experiencing was not peculiar to him but that all the people on the wing were also being hampered by the effects of 'neurotic extravagance'. Bion's attitude was both scientific and humanitarian, and was, as John Donne wrote, 'involved in mankind'. Donne had an understanding that his self, his being, was not separate from that of others but is part of a common substrate. This perception of the self was expressed by the seers who wrote the Upanishads over 2,500 years ago, and was shared by Bion, who wrote, 'The group is essential to the fulfilment of a man's mental life' (Bion 1961: 53).

The commander who issues the order that he is not to be interrupted from 10.00 a.m. to midday does not entertain the thought that he is just one of many suffering such frustration. His action does not have the status of a thought. He does not think at all. His action is motivated by the wish to be rid of this frustration and, remaining at the sensuous level, he does this through his order. It is inherent that other people do not feature within his emotional landscape. Bion's approach is different. He is frustrated but he observes himself, and the feeling of frustration reaches the status of a thought. Inherent in a thought is that it is the preserve of a relationship, that is, an 'open-ended reality in which there is no termination' (Bion 1992: 371). Bion's administrative action flows from a *thought* which is a product of the perception of his self in its reality of the selves of others. This is in contrast to the omnipotent self, which, with its sense of specialness, is an illusion and is not capable of emotional or mature thought. Thought is generated from the scientific, humanitarian self that is 'involved in mankind' and, inevitably, others are taken into account. We have gone into this is some detail because Pines is critical of Bion for not taking the individual into account. He asks:

why Bion did not see the group in the light of his model of the mother and child and their capacity to form a skilled pair. Bion was an amazingly perceptive observer of psychological phenomena but in his early work on groups he seemed to omit to account for the effects of his personality and technique on the situation that he was observing. He assumed that scientific and objective data could be obtained by the analytic instrument of the therapist's mind and that he needed only to test out the accuracy of his interpretations to have fulfilled his role as therapist. Bion had an impressive but remote personality, his remarks were often cryptic and difficult to understand, always addressed to the group as a whole, never directly to any one individual, however much an individual might long for direct contact with him. So for these persons Bion was not a mother whose reverie would return their urgent needs to them in a more digestible form. His technique fostered frustration and from the powerful forces of unleashed frustration develop the regressive group mentalities he so beautifully described.

(Pines 1987: 259)

We believe that Pines' opinion is such a radical misperception and one that is so widely shared that it is worth spending time on refuting it. His opinion fails to take into account that Bion's interpretations were based on respect for individual thinking. Bion clearly saw himself as one of the group participating both in the work mentality and in that of the basic assumptions. For example, periodically the group would accept that he was trying to show them something about themselves as a group. When this happened, Bion observed himself feeling relieved and with an immediate urge to open up to the group members, to give them something of what they wanted in the way of having a leader who would explain to them and thus allay their anxiety about this new experience. Having resisted this urge, which was the result of going along with the basic assumption of the dependent group, that is, becoming their leader on whom they could be dependent, he again found himself the object of group hostility.

His powers of observation and reflection were such that he was able to think about these experiences while he was in the midst of the group pressure and then communicate his thoughts to the group members. Bion's ability to think under 'battle conditions' is what we believe Pines mistakenly refers to as his remoteness.

At first Bion found himself beguiled into giving individual interpretations in an attempt, as he put it, 'to get individual treatment' (Bion 1961: 115) or doctoring for himself, by which he means getting rid of the badness. He recognized that the badness which he was trying to get rid of was the apparent unsuitability of the group as a therapeutic instrument. He realized, however, that the real trouble was his failure to use the group in a therapeutic way and that giving individual interpretations was a result of his being caught up in the group's basic assumption of dependency with him as leader, instead of supporting the work group mentality. He writes:

I very much doubt if any real therapy could result unless these psychotic patterns were laid bare with no matter what group. In some groups their existence is early discernible; in others, work has to be done before they become manifest. These groups resemble the analytic patient who appears much more ill after many months of analysis than he did before he had had any analysis at all.

(Bion 1961: 181)

Thus when Bion did not make an interpretation to the individual, it looked as if he was spurning the individual, but he was doing the opposite; he was recognizing the individuality of the other. Bion believes that the division between individual psychology and social psychology is based upon an illusion. Bion believed that what he felt in himself was shared by the members of the group. His group interpretation therefore strengthened the individuals in the group. We believe that Pines is mistaken in thinking that Bion was not concerned with the individual; rather, his concern was expressed differently from that of Pines.

At Northfield Bion introduced the following discipline:
1. Every man must do an hour's physical training daily unless a medical certificate excused him.
2. Every man must be a member of one or more groups – the groups designed to study handicrafts, Army correspondence courses, carpentry, map-reading, sand-tabling, etc.
3. Any man could form a fresh group if he wanted to do so, either because no group existed for his particular activity or because, for some reason or other, he was not able to join an existing similar group.
4. A man feeling unable to attend his group would have to go to the rest-room.
5. The rest-room would be in the charge of a nursing orderly and must be kept quiet. . . .

(Bion 1961: 15–16)

Also there was a 30-minute parade every day, the hidden but true purpose of which was to allow the men to view themselves in these activities.

Extravagant expression of neurosis was the group's enemy and a problem to be tackled by the group as a whole. At first sight it sounds as though this manner of action bore all the signs of a fight–flight group. There was a common enemy which the group fought. This enemy, however, was not located in the individual but rather was a disease of the whole group. Nevertheless, there was some element of the fight–flight mechanism in the centrality of a common enemy rather than the construction of a group ideal. Bion says explicitly that the model he used was that of a commander at war with a 'scallywag battalion' and a group at war typified the fight–flight group, as he later indicates when he is discussing specialized work groups. Let us say then that in the training wing of the Northfield Military Hospital he capitalized upon the fight–flight mechanism but raised it to that level where patients were encouraged to find the enemy within rather than the more primitive mechanism where it is projected into another who then is felt to *be* that enemy.

It was some six years later, in 1948, that the Tavistock asked Bion to take some therapeutic groups. He applied the same principle as at Northfield, that is, that what was expressed in the individual denoted a group configuration, and he set himself to study the group on this model. The person whose thoughts and feelings he knew best was himself. There is no difficulty in seeing the continuity between the group experiment at Northfield and the therapeutic groups which he took at the Tavistock. One may suspect, however, that his capacity to manage the projections of the group into him had become more deeply internalized. To be the object of powerful projections from the individual is difficult to bear, but the group magnifies the projections of the individual. Bion's capacity to manage the pressure put upon him by those first Tavistock groups and to survive well enough to make interpretations is, we believe, nothing short of heroic. Since his time many other analysts and therapists have taken groups according to his method, but to be the pioneer meant he had to tolerate also the fear that what he was doing might be mad. Since Bion, group therapists have had the authority of tradition to support them.

Before the Second World War Bion had had some analysis with Rickman. After the war Bion could not continue this arrangement as they had been involved in wartime psychiatric work together. In 1945 he went into analysis with Melanie Klein and would have been in analysis with her at the time when he was taking the groups at the Tavistock. We conjecture that the growth in his emotional capacity is attributable in part to his personal analysis with her. He gradually became convinced also of 'the importance of the Kleinian theories of projective identification and the interplay between the paranoid-schizoid and depressive positions' (Bion 1961: 8).

The specialized work groups are exemplified by the Army and the Church. These may have developed from the main societal group for the purpose of controlling and channelling the activity of basic assumption mentality of fight–flight and dependency respectively, so that these do not prevent the functioning of the work group. The Army provides an enemy and appropriate training against it, and the Church an idealized protective leader on whom all can depend. In these two institutions, therefore, we see the basic assumption mentality being constructively channelled into a work group. Certain activities are built in to these establishments to ensure that other basic assumption activities do not interfere with the smooth functioning of the group. For example, when a Church group has worked efficiently to achieve a substantial result, the Church quickly steps in to give thanks to God for allowing this achievement to occur, rather than give thanks to the work group which actually accomplished it. This is to ensure that the group remains dependent on a leader who cannot be made manifest and who therefore cannot lead in a more active way which may cause disruption of the status quo.

As mentioned above, as soon as Bion set to work at Northfield Military Hospital, he was inundated with requests from the men. This can be seen as the attempted formation of a basic assumption dependency group by the men, who were reluctant to take responsibility for themselves and were looking to Bion as the leader on whom they could be dependent for everything. He acted in the way a specialized work group would have done by reinstating the Army fight–flight mentality by defining a common enemy, neurosis.

Normally in a group, there are present together the work group and the dominant basic assumption group. In a specialized work group like the Church or the Army, the work group tries to ensure that the appropriate basic assumption remains dominant and is not interfered with by one of the other two basic assumption groups which might, by its emergence, lead to a disruption of the function of the whole organization. In a similar way, in the therapeutic group, the work group is present, together with one of the basic assumption groups which is dominant at that time. In this case, the readiness with which one basic assumption group can be replaced by another does not need to be guarded against, as with the Church or the Army; instead these changes can be used by the work group through observation and interpretation.

Arising from his observations in the Army and in these therapeutic groups, Bion viewed the condition of panic as related to the fight–flight mentality. He believed that the leader of a group in panic flight could easily turn the group around into a fighting unit; thus in panic, flight and aggression were interchangeable.

Bion noticed that when one basic assumption was present in the group the other two were absent, so he asked the question 'Where are they?' To answer this question he proposed the 'proto-mental system'. He suggested that there is a sort of substrate in the personality in which the bodily and the psychological are as yet undifferentiated. A bodily event as well as a psychological one can emanate from the proto-mental system. So an illness or mental suffering can be alternative signals from the system. The proto-mental system is neither mental nor physical but a state in which the two are undifferentiated. There is an obvious similarity between this theory and that of Hartmann, who believed that in early infancy the ego and the id are undifferentiated. In Hartmann's conceptualization the ego has not become differentiated at this stage so the personality is all drive or all instinct. With Bion an illness, an accident or a vocal utterance are all 'speech' of the proto-mental system. In his later thinking the proto-mental system was conceptualized as beta elements which may manifest themselves as accident, illness or vocal utterance. It is difficult to conceptualize a set-up in which the physical and the mental are not separate but one entity but this is what Bion postulates. When one basic assumption is operating in the group, the other two are excluded. They have been banished into the proto-mental system.

Bion thought that these basic assumptions were present not only in the small therapeutic group but also in those large mass groupings which make up society. He thought it might be possible to look at the matrix of disease processes using this idea of the proto-mental system.

Those basic assumptions which are within the proto-mental system are nevertheless still active, so that when, for example, a disease becomes overt physically, it will have psychological concomitants arising from the suppressed basic assumptions remaining in the proto-mental system.

Bion gives the example of tuberculosis occurring when a fight–flight basic assumption mentality is dominant in the community and the affiliated emotions are those of the suppressed dependency group. The treatment of tuberculosis consists of placing the tubercular patient in a position of considerable dependency, bed rest, or else minimal activity, isolation from the stresses of the world, and a diet which includes a lot of milk; in other words, a return of the adult to an infantile dependent state. This is the suppressed dependency basic assumption mentality expressing itself in association with the manifest disease.

One might hypothesize, for example, that the basic assumption dominating Western society at present is that of dependency, with its demand for more and more resources, far beyond its needs. The basic assumption mentalities of pairing and fight–flight are therefore suppressed in the proto-mental system, in that state in which physical and mental are as yet undifferentiated. A physical disease could arise which had affiliations with the emotions prevalent in the fight–flight or pairing groups. The cause of the illness would lie in the dominant basic assumption, that is, that of dependency. An illness which might fit this pattern and which has presented in epidemic form in the past few years is AIDS, with its overtones of an 'us against them mentality'.

Bion also thought that the fluctuations in the value of money might correlate with changing basic assumptions. He emphasizes that the relation between basic assumptions and disease or value of money is a reciprocal rather than a causal one. As rain, the oceans and evaporation are in a cyclical orbit rather than in a causal relation of one to the other, so also are the proto-mental system, the basic assumptions and diseases or changing value of money: 'when one basic assumption is being acted on the feelings associated with it are always linked with each other with the tenacity and exclusiveness, not more or less, that one would associate with chemical combinations' (Bion 1961: 95–6). So, for instance, resentment and frustration are indissolubly linked to the dependent group configuration. Bion proposed that his hypothesis be tested by a researcher using statistical methods.

It is necessary to add a footnote to what has been said about the proto-mental system. In the summary of his book *Experiences in Groups* Bion (1961: 189) says that he considers that the

primitive anxieties of part-object relationships contains the ultimate source of all group behaviour. Earlier on the same page he
says that the basic assumptions seem to be defensive reactions to
psychotic anxiety. Now is this a new theoretical position? Is it
compatible with his theory of the proto-mental system? Or is
it in conflict with it? There is little doubt that in this summary he
is trying to integrate his research and this theory both with Freud's
view of group behaviour and also with Melanie Klein's theory of
anxiety and part-object relationships. One thing is clear: that in
this summary he slips into an explanatory schema based upon a
causal relation rather than a reciprocal one. We believe therefore
that here he went against his own view in an attempt to
accommodate the views of Freud and Melanie Klein.

However, is the proto-mental system a composite of primitive
part-object relationships? And are primitive part-object relationships proto-mental? Are the physical and the mental indistinguishable in their constitution? We are inclined to the view that
this is the case because psychotic phenomena are manifest both
physically and psychologically. This provides evidence that the
proto-mental system is composed of primitive part-object relationships. The psychological *is* object-orientated.

Bion did not use the term 'proto-mental system' later in his
writing because it was replaced by that part of the mind which
was composed of 'beta elements'. His definition of 'beta elements'
fits exactly his description of the proto-mental system, namely:

> β-elements. This term represents the earliest matrix from which
> thoughts can be supposed to arise. It partakes of the quality
> of inanimate object and psychic object without any form of
> distinction between the two. Thoughts are things, things are
> thoughts; and they have personality.
>
> (Bion 1963: 22)

Bion's study of groups was a stepping-stone towards his mature
theory, which we have outlined in the previous chapters. The experience of analysis enabled him to clarify and enlarge his thinking. His
alpha functioning developed and was manifest in his mature theory.
The proto-mental system incorporating the basic assumptions was
beta elements. Bion himself was the mother in reverie assisting in
the process of transforming beta elements into alpha elements.
These alpha elements were in time transformed into concepts and
then a hypothetico-scientific system conceptualized in the Grid.

Bion's study of groups has become a classic and pioneered an approach to group psychotherapy which has continued at the Tavistock Clinic to this day. His methods have been severely criticized by some. However, Bion envisaged wider implications than group therapy alone. He was studying groups, how people function in groups and the groupishness in the individual before he or she meets up with others. He was looking for the wider implications of his theory.

In the psychotherapeutic or analytic couple, a group of two, we see the same ready tendency or valency to form basic assumption groups from the hopeful 'working well together' (pairing group) to the stuck sado-masochistic relationship (fight–flight). The dependency group is even more easily masked by the ready acquiescence of the analyst or therapist to being the benevolent one who 'knows best' and ends up taking the total responsibility for the work. The tendency to form groups is in all of us, including psychoanalysts and therapists.

Bion's *A Memoir of the Future* (1991) illustrates the multiple parts of the personality by displaying various groups of people meeting together. In these gatherings, in addition to attempts to understand meaning, we see the formation of basic assumption groupings which are against this work group activity. Bion conveys in this an idea of the group within the individual which opposes the work towards learning from experience and opening up the mind to the infinite thoughts waiting to be thought.

Dependent group culture is a manifestation of an unworked through Oedipus complex. When Freud first adumbrated this clinical entity he cast it in the paradigm of sexual craving of the child towards the parent of the opposite sex. The emotional rather than the sexual significance of this has been elucidated by later analysts. It has been stated most clearly by Erich Fromm:

> The full significance of Freud's discovery can be recognized only if we translate it from the sphere of sex into that of interpersonal relations. The essence of incest is not the sexual craving for members of the same family. This craving, in so far as it is to be found, is only one expression of the much more profound and fundamental desire to remain a child attached to those protecting figures of whom the mother is the earliest and most influential. The foetus lives with and from the mother, and the act of birth is only one step in the direction of freedom

and independence. The infant after birth is still in many ways part and parcel of the mother, and its birth as an independent person is a process which takes many years – which, in fact, takes a whole life. To cut through the navel string, not in the physical but in the psychological sense, is the great challenge to human development and also its most difficult task. As long as man is related by these primary ties to mother, father, family, he feels protected and safe. He is still a foetus, someone else is responsible for him. He avoids the disquieting experience of seeing himself as a separate entity charged with the responsibility for his own actions, with the task of making his own judgments, 'of taking his life in his own hands.' By remaining a child man not only avoids the fundamental anxiety necessarily connected with the full awareness of one's self as a separate entity, he also enjoys the satisfactions of protection, warmth, and of unquestioned belonging which he once enjoyed as a child; but he pays a high price. He fails to become a full human being, to develop his powers of reason and of love.

(Fromm 1972: 77–8)

Whereas Fromm has made a translation from sex to interpersonal relations, Bion has made a translation from the sexual to the emotional.

Chapter 13

The phenomenology of psychosis

How does the person know of pain ... so impalpable that its intensity, pure intensity, is so intense that it cannot be tolerated but must be destroyed even if it involves the murder of the 'anatomical' individual?

(Bion 1991: 51–2)

Bion wrote several papers on psychotic processes which were published between the years 1950 and 1958, that is, before the exposition of his new theories in the books *Learning from Experience, Elements of Psycho-Analysis* and *Transformations*. His work with psychotically disturbed patients was formative in his theory of thinking. His early papers on psychosis are published in *Second Thoughts*, together with his 'Commentary' on these papers written in 1967 after the publication of the above trilogy. In his Introduction to this book, when talking about detailed reports of sessions, Bion says,

> It has always seemed to me that such reports are open to the objection that the narrative and the interpretations given are only two different ways of saying the same thing or two different things said about the same fact. With the years my suspicion has ripened into conviction.

(Bion 1967: 1)

Every utterance is always a transformation and therefore the narrative and the interpretation are two different expressions of the same thing.

For Bion, thinking is a transformation. This is the essence of his theory of thinking, which is developed in the trilogy and finally expressed most fully in *Transformations*; namely that what transpires in the analytic session represents different transformations of the same emotional event, O. We have therefore left this chapter on psychosis to follow those which elaborate Bion's theory. The chapter focuses on Bion's observations during his initial work with psychotic and other severely disturbed patients, and makes links with the further elaborations of his theory.

When writing about psychotic patients, Bion refers not only to the overtly schizophrenic patient, with manifest thought disorder, but also to the psychotic part of the personality in borderline and neurotic patients. Thus the mechanisms described in psychotic patients do not comprise some esoteric theory but are for use in all patients, including oneself. The dominance of the psychotic part over the non-psychotic part in any personality interferes with mental functioning.

In these papers Bion speaks of verbal thought as the capacity which the psychotic achieves with difficulty and then hates because it gets him in touch with the reality of his psychic world. Bion conceptualizes pre-verbal thought as something like ideographs, mental pictures which would convey some aspect of reality, and which would be capable of joining together. With the development of his theory of thinking, these terms would be included under the whole apparatus of thinking, the ideographs being like visual images deriving from alpha elements.

SCHIZOPHRENIC LANGUAGE

In his paper 'Notes on the theory of schizophrenia', Bion describes the inappropriate use of language by the schizophrenic who, for example, uses it as a mode of thought when action would be more appropriate. For example, when a woman was going to buy meat, she found herself in the fish shop. She then believed that the fishmonger would sell meat to her. Language can be used as action; for example, in projective identification, to push words as things into the analyst, or, particularly when the analyst is felt to be persecuting, to split the analyst's mind giving rise in him to contradictory thoughts and conflicting interpretations.

We can see from these examples how the idea of the horizontal axis of the Grid may have occurred to Bion. Later he would see these uses of thought as action, as attempts by the psychotic part of the personality to interfere with a thinking relationship which might lead to change.

This paper and the one which follows it, 'Development of schizophrenic thought', focus on language and verbal thought in order to delineate the role of splitting and projective identification in attacking the apparatus of awareness required by the demands of the reality principle.

Having mutilated his apparatus of awareness, which is intimately related to the development of verbal thought, the schizophrenic feels himself imprisoned by his state of mind because he cannot escape it by the use of verbal thought, that is, he cannot verbalize his feelings, or name a constant conjunction which would enable meaning to develop. He has destroyed the key to his escape. During analysis, he begins to develop this capacity for verbal thought and effects his escape from his imprisonment. But he is now more aware of his feelings of painful depression, guilt and anxiety. He therefore splits off his newly acquired capacity for verbal thought and projects it into his analyst. Now, however, the lack of it makes him feel insane. Sometimes he believes that, Prometheus-like, he has been punished for daring to acquire it or else that the analyst has stolen it from him.

The achievement of a capacity for verbal thought is the turning point in the analysis, but Bion emphasizes that at this point the patient, now aware that he has hallucinations and delusions, will hate the analyst for bringing about this extremely disturbing awareness. He may try to reverse the process again by minute fragmentation.

Using Bion's theory of thinking, the acquisition of verbal thought would be subsumed under the development of the thinking apparatus in general. In the 'Commentary' Bion also says that he would now view the sense of imprisonment associated with the destruction of thinking processes in the light of $♀$ $♂$, with $♀$ crushing or imprisoning $♂$. The psychotic escapes from emotional pain only to be crushed by the $♀$ into meaninglessness and deathly rigidity.

In 'Notes on the theory of schizophrenia' Bion (1967a: 24) also claims that the counter-transference has to play an important part in the analysis of the schizophrenic. In his later works, however, he uses Freud's original definition of counter-transference, that 'which arises in the analyst as a result of the patient's influence on the analyst's unconscious feelings' (Freud 1971c: 144–5), and says repeatedly that counter-transference has no place in analysis; its only significance lies in the need for the analyst to have further analysis. This suggests a move away from the stance of 'What is this patient doing to me?' to a focus on the joint experience and the transformations of this.

THE SUPREMACY OF DEADLINESS

In his papers on psychosis, Bion emphasizes the importance, in the understanding of the schizophrenic, of the conflict that is never decided, between the life and death instincts (Bion 1967a: 38). Also he states that the 'schizophrenic is preoccupied with the conflict, never finally resolved, between destructiveness on the one hand and sadism on the other' (1967a: 37). This relates to the preponderance of destructive impulses, which is characteristic of the schizophrenic personality (1967a: 37), so that even loving impulses become imbued with them and are converted into sadism. This never-resolved conflict is thus an aspect of the psychotic part of the personality and contributes to the patient's feelings of hopelessness; renewed hope when the life impulses are dominant being undermined when the destructive and sadistic impulses reassert themselves, often apparently attacking or undoing any progress made. The crushing ♀ comes into action again.

A drug addict, after a great struggle, had weaned himself off drugs. He felt much more alive and able to think. He spoke of resuming his studies. On a Friday, his material had a banal quality, he appeared uninterested and detached, with neither interest nor pleasure in his development, nor anxiety about the future. The analyst nevertheless had an impression of his watchfulness and control. That night, he again took a heavy dose of drugs, abused his friends, and lost his job. Shortly before deciding to take the drugs he was aware of a feeling of loneliness which he found unbearable. This cycle was repeated with variations on many occasions. As soon as the life force asserted itself, painful as well as hopeful feelings were experienced. These could not be tolerated, at least in the initial stages, and the destructive side took over, overwhelming the precarious step forward and ready to destroy any progress. He also took pleasure in destroying what he thought was the analyst's hopefulness; in fact the arousal of hope is what is often sadistically attacked.

Bion emphasized in his later works that it is not only the fact that painful depressive emotions are aroused, but there is, in addition, a profound fear of change, of the unknown, of openness to a new experience.

After a period of destructiveness the life force again asserts itself, giving rise to further development, until challenged by the destructiveness. The transference relationship forms prematurely and is notable for both its tenacity and its thinness.

A patient early in his analysis said that the sessions made no difference to him; it was a matter of no consequence whether he came or not; that it was useful to him when the analyst took a break. This is an example of the thinness that Bion describes, but this patient was firmly attached to the analyst, evidence for this being his scrutiny of the analyst's expression as he came into the room, his close monitoring of the analyst in the session, his preoccupation with what the analyst thought, in addition to his interest when the analyst was mentioned at a party, his use of psychoanalytic words, reading books of psychological import and so on. But the results of all this did not increase emotional contact.

In his 1967 'Commentary' (1967a: 153), Bion describes the transference as constantly changing and he uses geometrical visual terms to describe these differences. A linear transference is one in which the link between analyst and patient is a line without breadth, but this tenuous and tenacious line is transformed in a moment into a monomolecular surface or plane. The patient seems to be in close contact with the analyst and this is seen in the transference. For example, one patient always picked up accurately his analyst's holiday destination. Another analyst felt a headache coming on immediately prior to a session. At the commencement of the session, the psychotic patient said, 'The children upstairs; it's enough to give you a headache.' But the transference is so thin that although the patient picks up various moods of the analyst, she does not discriminate between them, so that, for example, grief in the analyst would have no more significance than minor irritation.

As the patient attempts to broaden the transference relationship, he is assailed by confusional states which arise through the operation of projective identification which is overactive.

> Driven by the wish to escape the confusional states and harassed by the mutilations [of the dominant impulse by the temporarily subordinated instinct] the patient strives to restore

the restricted relationship; the transference is again invested with its characteristic featurelessness.

(Bion 1967a: 37)

Therefore an alternation between the restricted state and a more open state is typical of analysis when the psychotic part is dominant. This is seen when an awareness of psychic reality is achieved only to be followed by sessions characterized by lack of material.

HATRED OF PSYCHIC REALITY

As described in Chapter 7, the psychotic patient fears integration of thought because it will expose him to a dreaded aspect of himself of which he would prefer not to be aware, in particular, a savage super-ego. When there is a savage tyrant wreaking havoc within the personality, it makes sense that the individual does not want to know about it, and may be terrified of this primitive super-ego which attacks the self with relentless and vengeful criticism. A man was cut off from his feelings; it took some years of analysis before the reason emerged: that he felt as if he were in hell so he had to cut off the feelings in order to survive. But it was survival at a great cost: the inability to love or lead a fulfilled working life.

It is not, however, only the savage super-ego that the psychotic part fears. There is a hatred of reality both psychic and external and of anything which leads to awareness of it. In fact Bion was to state later in his life that he had never found much evidence of a super-ego, ego and id, meaning that he found evidence rather of a crushing, depleting morality, a ♀ that crushed life and liveliness. In his 'Commentary' in *Second Thoughts*, which was written about ten years after the papers on psychosis, Bion states that the psychotic patient 'appears to be peculiarly aware of, and persecuted by, psychic reality ... to the whole of psychic pleasure and pain' (Bion 1967a: 154). The psychotic has a particular difficulty in that from the beginning of life he seems prematurely to be aware that he is faced with having a psychic problem which cannot be dealt with merely by the provision of physical solutions; the pleasure–pain principle has to function in the endo-psychic world as opposed to being able to achieve satisfaction through the physical senses. We need to elaborate on this a little further. It is a paradox that the psychotic 'knows' that he has a problem which cannot be solved through marrying a suitable wife, having a satisfactory job, living in a pleasant neighbourhood, having sufficient money for a good standard of living. We presume that this knowledge resides in the non-psychotic part of the personality. It seems then that the pleasure–pain principle resides in the psychic world rather than in the sphere of physical senses. The implication here is that in the 'normal' person a different principle reigns in the psychic sphere, in other words, the reality principle. This reality, however, is that rooted in value; it is not to be equated with the inanimate world.

A child communicated something of this intolerable position to the analyst by first blowing as hard as he could into a baby feeding bottle, as though wanting to force feelings into the object to the point of bursting. Next, although it was a very hot day, he shut the windows, turned on the heater, making a revving sound as he twiddled with the knobs, as though revving a car. He told the analyst that a friend of his had revved her car so much that the temperature went right up to boiling point. As the heat in the room steadily rose, he said he was cold and huddled towards the heater. The analyst found the heat becoming suffocating, and wondered what to do as a sense of panic began to rise within her.

This conveys something of the helplessness and panic associated with having uncontrollable feelings which are experienced as being forced into one at an increasing rate, and not to know whether or when this process might stop. This is the experience of the psychotic with only the pleasure–pain principle available for dealing with the psychic world. He does not have the capacity for tolerance that would enable him to begin to think and thus relieve himself of some of the burden by thought.

The psychotic feels bombarded by stimuli building up inside him and with which he cannot cope. He feels the panic rise but he cannot stop the input, so he smashes his mental apparatus to demolish this experience. To obliterate this overwhelming psychic reality, the psychotic part destroys anything which might lead to awareness of it; any process leading to thought, and thus to the development of meaning, is destroyed. This includes everything embraced by the term 'alpha function', $\female$ $\male$ and the PS$\leftrightarrow$D mechanism, anything that has the function of linking two thoughts together. This destructive act takes place early in life and ensures that the development of the psychotic part will from then onwards be very different from that of the non-psychotic part.

Even the perceptual apparatus which provides material for thought processes may be attacked and destroyed, as may conscious awareness, attention, judgement and memory. These attacks are carried out with mutilating brutality and result in a smashing up into fragments or minute particles of the various aspects of the mind that make for an awareness of internal or external reality. The resultant particles are then violently projected out both into space and into external objects, which are felt to engulf them or else be engulfed by them. The patient feels himself to be surrounded by multiple, diverse, menacing objects. These smashing attacks on the mental apparatus and subsequent projection out of the fragments is the main feature which distinguishes the psychotic part of the personality from the non-psychotic part.

The projected-into objects, referred to by Bion as *bizarre objects*, each consist of the perceived external object into which the fragment of personality, combined with its particular function, has been expelled. This object seems to be as hostile or even more so than the force with which the hated fragment was expelled from the personality. Thus, if it was the function of vision which was expelled, then the engulfed or engulfing object is felt to be watching the patient with enormous hostility. The psychotic element is obvious when the object which is watching the patient malevolently is a cup, a photograph or a pair of glasses; it is much more concealed, however, when this object is another human being. For instance, someone who has expelled the function of vision may be convinced he is being watched malevolently by his mother, father, brother, sister, wife, children or neighbours. An analyst or therapist may often say that the patient's mother *was* insidious, that is, she was in reality as the patient describes. This disallows the possibility that there has been a projection of an attacking element into the mother and therefore the loss of a part of the self. Psychosis is frequently hidden in this way.

The reader will recall that reversal of alpha function results in the production of beta elements with traces of personality adhering to them. These are probably the same as the bizarre objects described above; thoughts revert into non-thoughts but with a menacing quality because of the hatred with which they have been ejected.

PSYCHOSIS: A DELUSIONAL WORLD

The explosion out of the mind of these particles of mental apparatus play a part in the formation of delusions which often crystallize out of a delusional mood, in which the environment, charged with these particles, is experienced as uncanny and threatening. The patient tries to use the bizarre objects in an endeavour to construct a meaning for his mental state, much as Freud described Schreber trying to reconstitute his world through his delusions. The presence in these bizarre particles of the patient's fragmented judgement gives a sense of conviction to a delusional perception.

The borderline or psychotic individual has a strong feeling that events in the outer world are personally related to him – ideas of self-reference. For example, a young adolescent, when watching television, thought that the announcer was speaking personally to her so that news items became of immense personal significance because they were the same as a part of her mind speaking to herself. Radio waves or the very atmosphere may be felt to be filled with minute hostile personal fragments and thus to be dangerous to the psychotic.

Bizarre objects cannot be linked together, they can only agglomerate. Bizarre objects are similar to or the same as beta elements. Although beta elements are not thoughts, they may have a tendency to become thoughts, their tropism, as previously mentioned. When describing the projection out of beta elements, Bion suggested that their dispersal might form a network resembling a prototype of $♀$, searching for something that would make them understandable, that is, coherent. They could also be seen as searching for a $♀$ and if they came across it, they could agglomerate to form the $♂$. If no $♀$ is found, however, the beta element network becomes more depressed-persecutory and greedy and threatening to the object that evacuated them.

Bion (1965: 137) also described delusions as occurring when a pre-conception mates with a realization but is not fully saturated by it because it does not match it closely enough; nevertheless, a conception or misconception is formed.

The fact that the psychotic individual cannot symbolize is related to this way in which external events acquire extreme personal significance to her because they contain fragments of functions of her own personality. Thus, certain external events are perceived as 'symbolic' to the psychotic. These are, in effect, pseudo-symbols in that they are not symbols that can be shared by others; rather they are attempts by the psychotic to make sense of her internal world. A well-known example of such a pseudo-symbol is from one of Bleuler's patients, who, believing she was pregnant, said, 'I hear a stork clapping in my body' (quoted in Fish 1962: 19). Sighting the 'baby-bringing' stork flapping its wings *is* her pregnancy.

Being surrounded by menacing bizarre objects, the patient lives in dread of imminent annihilation; thus her means for solving her initial problem of being in an almost intolerable situation has left her in an equally frightening state of mind. These objects, which to the non-psychotic are inanimate, confound the psychotic, to whom they appear endowed with life. They are a mixture of external objects and mental objects – ideas, senses and super-ego or ego functions such as attention and judgement. They also resemble anal objects, because of the phantasy of expelling them through the anus.

ATTACKS ON LINKING

Attacking the processes of thinking destroys the capacity for an awareness of external and internal reality. An efficient way of doing this would be by attacking any function that links up pre-verbal ideographs and their later developments that lead to verbal thought. Now we would see the link to be attacked as relating to any of the mechanisms of the thinking apparatus. The link which is attacked is that which productively joins any couple; for example, that between mother and infant, between analyst and patient, between parts of the self, or between pre-conception and realization. In his paper 'Attacks on linking' (1967a) Bion gives examples of attacks on the parental couple, attacks on the very language of communication as in a stutter, and attacks on primitive projective identification, the link between the young infant and the mother, on the success of which depends his mental development. This particular link may be enviously attacked by the infant, who cannot bear the mother's peace of mind, that is, her ability to tolerate the painful feelings projected into her by the same infant.

In the 'Commentary' Bion goes on to say that the psychotic patient tries to attack the potential link between analyst and patient by attempting to saturate the analyst's pre-conceptions, for example by stimulating memory or desire in the analyst, so that his pre-conceptions are no longer available for matching up with the appropriate realization. They are already saturated by the 'sense' of memory and desire (Bion 1967a: 162).

With destruction of the link, two objects cannot be brought together in a productive way, the prototype of which is a commensal ♀ ♂ mechanism from which is produced something of mutual benefit. Thus symbol formation, in which two objects are brought together to reveal their similarity (the invariant) but retain their separate identity, becomes difficult. For example, a cat with its ability to slip in and out of a house could be a symbol of slipping into the mind of another. To a psychotic youth who saw a cat on the way to his analytic session, this was proof that he had already slipped inside his analyst's mind.

When this attack on linking takes place, the links are fragmented and projected out, resulting in the patient being surrounded by minute cruel links which can join bizarre objects together but with cruelty.

The excessive and violent expulsion also interferes with smooth introjection and assimilation necessary to provide a firm base for the establishment of verbal thought. The expulsion is experienced as an intrusive process of varying degrees of violence which interferes with the flow of material during a session. This is another attack on linking.

This was illustrated by a psychotic boy who would take the soft cushion out of its firm cover and nurse it like a baby, gently rocking it and speaking soothingly to it, only to suddenly shout at it, demonstrating how it then shook with fear. This had been preceded by months of sessions during which sudden and unexpected assaults would be made on the analyst, resulting in an apprehensive state of mind which interfered with calm receptiveness: in terms of Bion's theory of thinking, it interrupts the process whereby a realization might match up with a pre-conception, the container–contained relationship which would lead to the establishment of something reliable. This is the particular link attacked.

The psychotic part disrupts any interaction which might result in insight on the analyst's part because this threatens change and emotional pain. For example, in an analysis many days would pass before the analyst got insight into the problem. Then one of two things would happen: either the patient obliterated entirely from his mind the interpretations and associations of that session, or he would cancel the following session, thereby interrupting the flow of understanding. This is another example of attacking a link because it was at the point that the analyst was integrating the disparate elements.

This disruptive process can also be expressed in motor action such as abruptly sitting up on the couch, walking out of a session, or refusal to speak, by trying to draw the analyst into a collusion, for example a sado-masochistic one, or more subtly in the content or manner of speech which fills the analyst with information but conveys nothing evocative. All these outer activities of which the analyst is the receptor are symbolic of inner actions directed against the patient's own mind.

ARROGANCE, CURIOSITY AND STUPIDITY

Another example of attacks made on a particularly important link is given in the paper 'On arrogance'. Bion realized that certain uses of projective identification were to ensure emotionally rewarding experiences, such as putting bad parts of the self into the object so that they could be rendered more tolerable, and projecting good parts, resulting in an idealized object: 'Associated with these experiences was a sense of being in contact with me, which I am inclined to believe is a primitive form of communication that provides a foundation on which, ultimately, verbal communication depends' (Bion 1967a: 92). It is the means by which the infant communicates his emotional state to his mother. Her ability to tolerate and process these feeling states, especially the frightening ones, enables the infant to take them back in a manageable form and also gradually to introject this capacity to process emotional experiences. If the maternal object is not receptive to these projections and will not allow them entry, she is experienced as not being able to stand this method of communication and therefore as being hostile to the baby's attempts to think. This is a disastrous situation for the baby, who presumably feels thwarted in his very attempts to make sense of his world. Out of this develops a hostile super-ego with particular qualities, including that of denying the use of projective identification, that is, of impermeability. This sort of super-ego is present in borderline and psychotic patients.

A similar situation was revealed in a patient in whom Bion observed a constant conjunction of curiosity, stupidity and arrogance. In this paper Bion defines arrogance as follows: 'The meaning with which I wish to invest the term "arrogance" may be indicated by supposing that in the personality where life instincts predominate, pride becomes self-respect, where death instincts predominate, pride becomes arrogance' (Bion 1967a: 86). For Bion, Oedipus' reckless pursuit of the truth under the sway of the death instinct is an example of such 'arrogance'.[1] He views this as a central issue, thus lending a new perspective to the myth. Oedipus did not have the capacity to cope with the truth he found; it aroused his destructive impulses rather than reparative ones.

Pursuit of the truth in analysis at no matter what cost is felt to imply a claim to be able to receive and contain any projective identifications without losing one's peace of mind. This claim invites hatred and envious attacks.

In working with a particular patient who showed a marked negative therapeutic reaction, Bion observed that in the clinical material there were scattered manifestations of curiosity, stupidity and arrogance. This is an example of a constant conjunction, which, having been noted and named, eventually yielded the meaning of a primitive psychological disaster.

He describes the repeatedly thwarted attempts at verbal intercourse between him and a particular patient. Sometimes the obstruction appeared to be in him, sometimes in the patient and sometimes in between. Some clarification occurred when the patient identified the analyst as the obstructing force together with the idea that he, the analyst, could not stand 'it'.

Meanwhile there were repeated references to curiosity and stupidity which seemed to increase or decrease in parallel. In his later 'Commentary' on 'On arrogance', Bion says that it is essential that the operation of the curiosity be demonstrated; its name is not the significant point. In other words, it is the conjunction of these traits in action that is important rather than their being mentioned by name. Arrogance occurred in various forms and with different names. Later it became apparent that what the object, at that time the analyst, could not stand was the patient's

---

[1] The *Oxford English Dictionary* definition of arrogance is making or implying unwarrantable claims to dignity, authority or knowledge; aggressively conceited, haughty or overbearing.

method of communication, which was not verbal but was, instead, by projective identification. The patient felt that the analyst, by using verbal communication, was attacking his methods of communication.

The obstructive object was felt to be curious about him but hostile to his method of communication, that is, projective identification. The object accordingly made destructive, mutilating attacks on this through varieties of stupidity, that is, the object made itself appear too stupid to understand the projected experience. The result of this was a psychological disaster because of the destruction of this primitive link between them. Another outcome was the development of a primitive super-ego which denied the use of projective identification.

These processes were demonstrated in a patient who manifested intense curiosity about the analyst's appearance, clothes and publications but who retreated from any transference insight, claiming that she did not want to know anything about that. She did not feel understood and the analyst felt she blocked out his interpretations. She manifested considerable arrogance in her attitude to her associates at work and at times to the analyst. Some sessions would pass with virtually no dialogue, during which the analyst might become aware of terrified infantile feelings as of being about to fall from a height, indicating the pre-verbal anxieties blocked from expression for so long.

This primitive disaster of the attack on the communicative value of projective identification may remain hidden in a state of apparent impasse.

DEVELOPMENT OF THE SAVAGE SUPER-EGO

The savage super-ego arises in the following way. When the external object fails to accept the baby's projections, it is felt to be hostile to the baby's attempts to explore it. If the external object is felt to be understanding, it arouses the infant's envy and hatred, resulting in the object being transformed into a greedy and envious object which voraciously takes in emotional experiences and denudes them of goodness. Rather than making them tolerable by giving them meaning, the objects are left in a degenerate state. The infant receives back from the mother a meaningless and intensified fear. This results in the establishment within the infant of a structure not only hostile to projective identification but also deliberately misunderstanding it. Alpha function is not established, the infant cannot become aware of himself and cannot use perceptions to render the world meaningful. His rudimentary consciousness therefore cannot cope and in addition he has the above internal object or super-ego which aims at misunderstanding communication and experience.

THE PSYCHOTIC ATTEMPTS TO THINK

The psychotic uses words in an unusual way, not as the name of the phenomenon, that is, the thing as it appears to the observer, nor yet as the thing-in-itself, which is the thing as it is supposed to be in reality without the observer, that is, that which cannot be known. Instead he uses the word as though it were identical with the thing-in-itself; in other words, he understands the thing-in-itself as being the same as an idea, so that if the object talked about is acted upon in some way, the psychotic patient thinks that his mind is being interfered with.

Although the psychotic patient does not want to experience the agonizing awareness of his reality, his solution has resulted in him now being imprisoned in a state of mind from which he can obtain no satisfaction; he can no longer make sense of his world, he has lost his capacity to be aware of reality, he cannot dream or get to the stage of using symbols. He has destroyed the means by which he could become aware of himself and think his way out.

The psychotic tries to use bizarre objects as ideas, thoughts or words and fails to understand why they cannot be manipulated in this way. In trying to think, he endeavours to bring them back inside himself. As he cannot introject properly, he must bring them back by an exact reversal of the manner in which he evacuated them. He feels therefore that the aspects of himself imbedded in the multiple external bizarre objects have to be forced back inside him through the same body orifice by which, in phantasy, they were expelled. Owing to the fact that the links have been destroyed, these expelled fragments, when taken back, cannot be articulated. Instead they are agglomerated, compressed or fused and any joining is done with a vengeance, since they were expelled with hatred. They may therefore be experienced as physically painful hallucinations.

A borderline psychotic boy, when spoken to of his despair about ever being recognized or loved, shouted out that his analyst was not sitting next to him but was getting up his bum. He experienced the analyst's words as painful things that were being pushed into his bottom rather than into his ears or mind. As indicated above, the psychotic uses words as if they were concrete objects rather than as signs for a constant conjunction of ideas. He violently threw out painful aspects of himself, in this case agonizing feelings aroused by being understood. Their impetus to return was felt as hard, painful things which his analyst was trying to force back into him, perhaps also with connotations of a sexual assault. Bion says, 'whether [the patient] feels he has had something put into him, or whether he feels he has introjected it, he feels the ingress as an assault, and a retaliation by the object for his violent intrusion into it' (Bion 1967a: 40–1).

INTOLERANCE OF FRUSTRATION

The psychotic part is intolerant of frustration, therefore the processes (alpha function) which would lead to thoughts and thinking are not activated, indeed alpha function is destroyed or reversed. Instead of emotional experiences becoming meaningful, they are depleted of their meaning; the container–contained mechanism functions to destroy meaning rather than to promote mutual growth. As mentioned above, already formed alpha elements are turned back into something resembling beta elements, but with aspects of the personality adhering to them, for example frightening qualities associated with anal objects, or the super-ego. These personalized beta elements are bizarre objects.

A woman was able to understand an interpretation and there was a sense of co-operation between her and the analyst, but next day the analyst had been turned into a monstrous Nazi-like sadist who spoke to her only to hurt and undermine her. She had also felt attacked and belittled at work. Reversal of alpha function had occurred and the analyst and her work fellows had been turned into bizarre objects.

The above processes, the workings of the psychotic part of the personality, result in disorders of thought, destruction of meaning, abnormalities of perception, including hallucinations, and personality deterioration. Disorders of thought are the imprisoned patient's attempts to communicate, having destroyed the means by which this communication with the self and others normally occurs. In addition, he is frightened by the menacing presence of the bizarre objects and is in dread of annihilation.

During analysis, the psychotic patient may wish to communicate with the analyst, but he cannot do so by the usual verbal means as he has severely damaged his capacity for verbal thought. What he wishes to communicate cannot be named; instead it is has to be intuited by the analyst through whatever means the patient can provide. This can be achieved through elaborate bodily movements or by using an image or ideograph, which he may have had stored in memory for some considerable time. This ideograph may be used to convey a multiplicity of meanings. It is not a symbol but an agglomeration of mental facts which the patient wishes to convey to the analyst. It can be done with great skill (see Chapter 10).

OTHER CLINICAL PROBLEMS

In analysing a schizophrenic Bion says that it is necessary to manufacture the mental apparatus required as one goes along. Models cannot be used, so it is like having to work out a problem using the original object, instead of having the aid of some substitute which one can manipulate. Models cannot be used because the psychotic thinks so concretely that he confuses the model with reality.

For example, a psychotic adolescent boy threw some toy animals off the table and then said that he could not hear any noises from upstairs, where he believed a children's school was held. He believed that by throwing out the animals, he concretely got rid of the children not only from above but also from his mind and that of the analyst. An interpretation which said that by throwing the animals away he was showing how he wanted to get rid of that which aroused jealousy from his mind or that of the analyst, like throwing out unwanted rubbish, would not have been understood. He concretely believed that he had done so.

While a more neurotic patient can make allowances for interpretations which are not completely accurate and can fill in the gaps, as it were, to bridge the inaccuracy, the psychotic patient can accept only very accurate interpretations and will do so often in a very concrete way. Sometimes it is extreme sadism towards the analyst that prevents him accepting any interpretations that are not completely right. The sadistic element rejoices in the mistaken aspect of the interpretation and so eliminates it; the patient cannot tolerate an interpretation that may not be quite right but is 'on the right track', to use a phrase of Bion's.

A patient may also listen very closely to the tone of the analyst's voice and may only register this, not the verbal content. If the analyst's tone is irritated, a neurotic may register this fact but is able nevertheless to accept the interpretation; the psychotic patient, however, believes that the interpretation was made in order to use him as a receptacle for the analyst's unwanted mental content.

By remaining unaware of the selected fact which would promote the PS↔D move, the psychotic part stops integration but the individual is left with feelings of persecution for which he attempts to find a cause. This attempt, as well as any 'cause' found, is a column 2 phenomenon, because it is an attempt to prevent emergence of the truth, namely that the persecutory feelings are associated with a refusal to allow their integration. This attempt is seen in the patient, who, having become aware of destructive hatred towards the analysis, asks why he should be like this, and searches hopefully for facts in his upbringing which caused this aspect of himself which he would like to repudiate.

When confronted by the psychotic part of the personality, it is necessary to clarify with the patient the defects in these areas, the way in which the thinking apparatus is malfunctioning. For example, the container–contained apparatus may be functioning in such a way as to destroy meaning rather than to increase it, or the Oedipal pre-conception may have been shattered so that inter-pretations at an Oedipal level embracing the concept of parental intercourse will not be understood.

HALLUCINATIONS

Hallucinations are vivid sensory mental impressions without an adequate external stimulus. Bion believed that they are produced by the sense organs functioning in reverse: the eyes, as it were, excrete a visual impression, the ears, an auditory impression, and the same for the sense of smell, touch and taste. If a borderline or psychotic patient says that he sees something, it may be that he is not perceiving an external object but rather that he is hallucinating.

In the middle of a session a young woman with borderline psychotic symptoms would suddenly look away to the side or up to the ceiling, open her eyes wide while pulling down the corners of her mouth in a grimace, and then appear to be involved in animated conversation with two or more people. She would appear to be listening with avid interest, her face assuming a condescending and animated expression, as though she were running a successful soirée. The analyst felt completely left out and of no use. The complete absorption with which she engaged in this activity and the intensity of her looking and listening gave the impression that she was hallucinating. The sensual conviction given by the hallucination contributed considerably to her absorption and satisfaction. In this exciting world where she was the centre of attention, what need had she of an analyst or of anyone else?

These may be considered obvious hallucinations but Bion makes the point that 'until co-operation evolves, there is no question of "observing hallucinations"' (Bion 1967a: 158). He also says that it is difficult to specify how the analyst becomes aware that hallucination is occurring but it is a situation that evolves in the session; when, for example, what was at one moment experienced as an outpouring of hostility towards the analyst suddenly comes away like a skin floating off and in the new state, the analyst recognizes that the patient is hallucinating. In his 'Commentary' Bion emphasizes that in order to experience the evolution of these states of mind, for example of hallucinosis, it is important that the analyst try to achieve that state of mind in which pre-conceptions are left unsaturated, that is, of abstention from memory and desire. Hallucination is probably much commoner than is realized. For example, a hallucinated figure is a common feature in adolescent girls with severe eating disorders (Magagna 1994).

The study of hallucinations also sheds light on the peculiarity of dreams in the psychotic patient. Initially there are no dreams, as though the material that might have been processed into a dream is so fragmented that it is like mental urine, which seeps away and is lost from the mind. Such patients do not bring dreams until, in the analysis, there is some move towards the depressive position and the beginnings of the development of whole objects. When, in the course of an analysis, such a patient begins to dream, he cannot distinguish this from an hallucination and thinks that he has actually taken inside himself the person of the analyst and is now in the process of excreting him in the dream. This is a very distressing situation and can result in the patient either becoming suicidal or else retreating from the more coherent state which has given rise to the suicidal depressive feelings; he re-fragments his material in such a massive way that there is no possibility of the fragments ever being brought together again. The renewed danger of suicide when the patient begins to make a recovery from his depressed state is well known in the practice of psychiatry; this may be the moment when the fragments have come together enough to convince the patient that he has destroyed his object, now perceived as a whole object. The other danger is the irreparable secondary fragmentation.

Because of the change in the nature of hallucinations when there has been some progress in terms of movement into the depressive position, Bion made a distinction between hallucinations of whole objects associated with depression and those of fragments; the latter he termed psychotic hallucinations and the former hysterical hallucinations, but both occur in the psychotic patient. A woman saw 'bits' on the analyst's wall, for instance a nose over the doorway. These were hallucinatory fragments. She also on one occasion believed that the analyst *was* her boyfriend. This was an hysterical hallucination.

The psychotic patient's fear of committing murder is partly that he thinks he has already done so; in this case, the life has been taken out of the object and projected into an external object, which may then be experienced, for example, as emitting electricity or dangerous wave-forms or rays. The latter represent the stolen life-force and sexuality. He can avoid experiencing guilt by feeling persecuted by the destroyed object instead. As he is in that state of mind which is dominated by an intolerance to frustration and an impulse to expel immediately any uncomfortable feeling, this lends weight to the hallucinatory discharge, which is experienced as an unburdening of the psyche, with the aid of muscular action, such as a facial grimace. The muscular action, of whatever nature, gives force to the idea of a murderous attack, that is, a real action has occurred motivated by feelings of hate and envy.

If he has a feeling of love which he wishes to express to a girl, he feels frustrated in his attempt because he believes he has been deprived by his parents of what he needs to make him potent in this regard, for example a potent penis. He is filled with envy, resentment and murderous rage which he cannot tolerate. He then assaults someone or something in an attempt to disburden himself of these feelings. It may only be a token assault but it has the effect of explosively evacuating these aspects and scattering them into a variety of objects. He is thus now free to love but is left relatively denuded of feelings and surrounded by murderously hating bizarre objects.

If a patient transforms his emotional experience into hallucinations, he feels he has got rid of a problem, especially that of dependency on another. With his ability to hallucinate, he believes he can manufacture whatever he needs. Neither does he have to wait or depend on anyone else. Greed can be everlastingly satisfied. This attitude can be maintained so long as he can avoid contact with reality. This produces a particular problem in analysis in that the patient believes that the solution to his problems lies in hallucination, which is felt to be superior to the analyst's solution, namely interpretations and their consequences. When the patient's solution fails to bring the expected satisfaction, then he believes that the analyst, out of envy, rivalry and greed, has stolen the satisfaction from his hallucinations and is feeling superior to him. The analysis, from the patient's point of view, thus becomes converted into a situation between rivals, one or the other becoming 'superior'. This needs to be interpreted so that the disagreement is returned to the intrapsychic sphere, between the psychotic and the non-psychotic parts of the patient's personality. In addition, the analyst's interpretations may be experienced as a discharge of unwanted material, just as the patient achieves such a discharge with his hallucinations.

This can be seen as a –K situation, dominated by the presence of objects denuded of their meaning, and associated with a sense of moral superiority. This is maintained by the psychotic part of the personality, which is also manifested in the group, without or within, when the group members are filled with a sense of conviction expressed in the clause 'We know' or 'We know best'.

The final paper in *Second Thoughts* is on Bion's theory of thinking, the development and growth of thoughts, as has been outlined in this book.

Bion begins his paper with a prejudiced viewpoint:

In this paper I am primarily concerned to present a theoretical system. Its resemblance to a philosophical theory depends on the fact that philosophers have concerned themselves with the same subject matter; it differs from philosophical theory in that it is intended, like all psycho-analytical theories, for use.

(Bion 1967a: 110)

It is of course true that much philosophy exists in a vacuum, but good philosophy has always been generated to solve real problems that have arisen in the midst of humankind's social world. It is also the case that many psychoanalytical theories only have a dysfunctional use in that they impede analytic understanding. It is the only instance that we are aware of in Bion's writings where he betrays an idealization of psychoanalysis. Nor does he correct this viewpoint in his 'Commentary'.

He states that the apparatus available to the psyche may be regarded as fourfold:

1 Thinking, associated with modification and evasion.
2 Projective identification, associated with evasion by evacuation and not to be confused with normal projective identification.
3 Omniscience (on the principle of *tout savoir tout condamner*).
4 Communication

(Bion 1967a: 117)

OMNISCIENCE AND OMNIPOTENCE

If the personality is intolerant of frustration but not so intolerant that it has to evacuate the experience from the mind, omnipotence develops as a substitute for waiting for the appropriate realization to mate with the pre-conception. There is an omniscient assertion that this is the truth. There is no learning from experience what is true and what is not.

> Omniscience substitutes for the discrimination between true and false a dictatorial affirmation that one thing is morally right and the other wrong. The assumption of omniscience that denies reality ensures that the morality thus engendered is a function of psychosis.

(Bion 1967a: 114)

COMMUNICATION

Bion's use of the term 'publication' refers not only to the intrapsychic task of making the sensory impressions available to the individual's consciousness but also to making one's private thoughts public. The latter obviously involves the ability to express one's thoughts in the appropriate language for communication but also involves an internal conflict between the individual's narcissism and his social-ism or allegiance to the group of which he is inevitably a part. Bion says, 'the human animal ... cannot find fulfilment outside a group and cannot satisfy any emotional drive without expression of its social component' (Bion 1967a: 118). Communication is by projective identification, originally used in infancy to communicate emotional states, and which, if successful, results in the ability to tolerate psychic qualities. This type of projective identification, as opposed to that which is distorted by omnipotent phantasies, is used to communicate from one individual to another. The sense of persecution that may arise in the recipient of this method of communication tends to be dealt with by resorting to abstraction, to distancing from the immediacy of the emotional component. It is also the method of communication in groups, an example of which is Bion's basic assumption group, in which the psychotic element is communicated in this way. Presumably emotional states other than psychotic ones can also be communicated by the same method.

Communication with oneself involves the correlation of data from different sensory modalities to produce a common-sense view. If these data harmonize, a sense of truth is experienced which is necessary to nourish the mind. Psychic reality deals with emotional data rather than sensory data, and in this case correlation may result in a common emotional view of a particular object. If the different views of the object are conjoined and there is confirmation that the two or more differently held emotions are directed towards the same object, then a sense of truth is experienced.

Chapter 14

Without memory or desire

He who binds to himself a joy
Doth the winged life destroy;
But he who kisses the joy as it flies
Lives in Eternity's sun rise.

(Blake 1972: 179)

One of Bion's most controversial recommendations was that the analyst should approach the session without 'memory or desire'. At the International Congress of Psycho-analysis in 1975 in London, Leo Rangell, who was immediate past President, opposed this recommendation by saying that if he were to approach an analytic session in this vein he would not feel justified in charging a fee.

At a moment in a session the analyst understands that behind an array of pompous bullying his patient is suffering intense shame. Now the question is 'How does that understanding arise in the analyst?' There is a directness of experience which was not there before. Shame, as an emotional reality, is now within the analyst's emotional orbit. It is no longer confined within the boundaries of the patient's psyche. The analyst does not know it as he might know the day of the week, the depth of the Thames or the number of siblings in the patient's family. The shame confronts his emotional being. If this shame is not outside him then it is apprehended as a reality within him. He apprehends that reality because he has become it in the depths of his being. The seeing of the shame comes about as a result of a transformation. In other words a piece of insight of this kind is a sign of the emergence of a new reality in the depths of his being but it is also an indication of a cognate change in the patient.

Now what are we talking of when we speak of a new reality? Bion says that this is the emergence of the truth. He used the term O to designate the truth or ultimate reality. O is not known directly but in that moment when the analyst sees the shame there is an indirect apprehension of O. This happens by becoming O, of which the 'seeing' is the transformation. Bion designates this as $K \rightarrow O$.

Seeing shame then designates the emergence of O, but shame is 'seen' or *intuited*, to use Bion's term. Shame in itself is not something that is perceived through the senses. You may see someone blushing and infer the presence of shame but you cannot see the shame itself. The case where you see someone blushing and infer shame is quite different to the one where the analyst *intuits* shame. In the one case it is outside and in the other the analyst has *become* it. A psychic reality is only known by being 'become' first. What we have said of shame goes for grief, joy, envy, love, hatred, gratitude, meanness, anxiety and all the emotions.

Now Bion says that the psychic reality can only be known through intuition. This means that the mental-emotional reality is apprehended directly and not via the senses. Bion's proposition is that the senses block intuition of the psychic reality. Now both memory and desire are rooted in the senses and therefore they both block our intuition of psychic reality. Intuition does not occur through sense perception. Instead those moments of insight occur through an inner creative act of thought. Such moments have been studied carefully in Koestler's book *The Act of Creation* (1975) and also in Bernard Lonergan's book *Insight* (1958). The classic instance of such insight was the experience of Archimedes, whose master, King Hieron, tyrant of Syracuse, had set him the task of finding out whether his recent gift of a crown was made of pure gold or whether there was some admixture of a baser metal, such as silver. Archimedes knew the specific weight of gold, which means he knew the weight of gold per volume-unit, but his problem was to find out the volume of the crown with all its complicated decoration and filigree work. If he could melt it down and reduce the shape to that of a brick, his problem would be easily solved, but how to discover its volume while leaving the crown intact? One day at the public baths, while lowering his body into the water, he realized in a flash that the volume of his body was equal to the quantity of water displaced. He now knew he could weigh the crown and find the volume of gold which it equalled. He could get a gold bar of that weight, put it in the water and measure the amount of water displaced, then put the crown into the water and, if it was pure gold, it would have to displace the same amount of water. As is well known, when Archimedes 'saw' this he ran through the streets of Syracuse shouting 'Eureka! Eureka! ... I've got it, I've got it!'

Now this act of insight occurs through the algebraic use of a symbol for volume. The insight that the volume of the body equals the volume of water displaced can be written as an equation:

$$V * b = V * wd$$

where V = volume; b = body and wd = water displaced. Now volume is not something that can be seen. If you pointed to a large man and then to a large bucket of water and said to a 5-year-old child that they are the same he would think you were mad. Volume is a mental reality. Yet Archimedes' insight was only possible through possession of the reality which we name volume. His act of insight occurs in the moment of transition from the visual reality (namely his body and the water) to the mental reality (namely volume) where water displaced and body = the same volume.

Commenting on the emotional state in which this happens, Lonergan says,

> Insight comes suddenly and unexpectedly. It did not occur when Archimedes was in the mood and posture that a sculptor would select to portray 'The Thinker'. It came in a flash, on a trivial occasion, in a moment of relaxation.

(Lonergan 1958: 4)

The state of relaxation or *reverie*, to use Bion's word, or *free-floating attention*, to use Freud's term, is that which best disposes the mind to make that transition from sensual to mental. To be attached to the sensual prevents that transition from one to the other and therefore blocks understanding. Bion makes it clear that it is not the memory as such that blocks understanding but rather the attachment to it. What Bion recommends is that the analyst place on himself a discipline where he detaches himself from an addictive attachment to memory. Bion says that it is the psychological state of attachment to the sensual that needs to be relinquished. He says, for instance, that there can be just as injurious an attachment to 'forgetting': 'I do not mean that "forgetting" is enough: what is required is a positive act of refraining from memory and desire' (Bion 1970: 31). If, for instance, in the state of reverie a memory floats into the mind of the analyst, then that memory *as a symbol of a psychic reality* is extremely relevant. It is the state of mind which is crucial here. What Bion is recommending is very closely allied to what Buddhists refer to as *Nirodha*. *Nirodha* means the cessation of thirst for all that is transient. The Buddha said we have to strive for the cessation of *dukkha*. *Dukkha* has often been translated as 'suffering', but this is not correct. *Dukkha* means rather that attachment to the transient aspects of this world that brings about suffering. That attachment is known as *tanha*, which means 'thirst' for the sensual things of life. Most often this is thought of in terms of food, drink and other such pleasures of life. However, it is also attachment to inner imaginative impressions and it is our clinical observation that these hidden attachments have a much greater pull over the psyche than outer physical things. To describe this state of mind after which the analyst must strive Bion uses the term *Negative Capability*, a term coined by Keats. Bion quotes this passage from a letter which Keats wrote to his brothers:

> I had not a dispute but a disquisition with Dilke on various subjects; several things dove-tailed in my mind, and at once it struck me what quality went to form a Man of Achievement, especially in Literature, and which Shakespeare possessed so enormously – I mean Negative Capability, that is, when a man is capable of being in uncertainties, mysteries, doubts, without any irritable reaching after fact and reason.
>
> (Bion 1970: 125)

Bion's recommendation that the analyst strive after Negative Capability is not an immediate mental discipline to be engaged in just prior to the session, but rather a way of life.

There is an equation between reverie and psychic reality as if when the mind wanders from its attachment to the specific perceptual reality it makes that transition to psychic being whose reality is known through symbols, the manipulation of which allows the act of insight.

The difference between the problem which Archimedes had set himself and that of the psychoanalyst is that the data out of which the latter draws his problem is emotional experience whereas with the former it is the physical realities of the external world, but the process is similar in that the act of understanding occurs in the transition from the sensual to the psychic. Bion's point is that memories and desires are rooted in the sensual whereas understanding occurs through the symbolic identity in psychic reality. We started this chapter with an example of how the psychic reality of shame emerged into the analyst's mind. We can assert with certainty that these insights occur in a way that is similar to the way in which insight came to Archimedes. We take first an example from Freud. In 'The ego and the id', where he is discussing how unconscious realities become conscious, he suddenly says:

> it dawns upon us like a new discovery that only something which has once been a *Cs.* perception can become conscious, and that anything arising from within (apart from feelings) that seeks to become conscious must try to transform itself into external perceptions.
>
> (Freud 1971d: 20)

The realization that hits Freud is that consciousness is of the external perceptions and that inner realities have to transform themselves into this in order to become conscious. Here the insight is based upon a realization of the ontological difference between inner realities and external perceptions. When we were discussing Archimedes we noted that the insight lay in the psychic reality which was identical in the two cases – that is, the body and the water displaced – and the same is so here: there is an invariant in the unconscious reality and in the conscious one upon which the insight relies. The intuition grasps the invariant under the two different forms. We produce this example, however, to indicate the different sort of data that Freud was working with from Archimedes, but, at the same time, how the process of insight is according to the same principles. We can see also many insights in Bion. For instance where he uses the image of binocular vision – that is, a combination of unconscious and conscious mentation – for the mind to be able to appreciate psychic quality. He is stressing here the moment of insight occurring in the conjunction of the inner and outer reality. Both with Freud and Bion the data being processed are emotional experience.

This is also why Bion came to the view that desire for the cure of the patient was an obstacle to the analysis. Cure or healing is a by-product of the process of analysis. Bion says, 'The tendency to equate psycho-analysis with "treatment" and "cure" with improvement is a warning that the psycho-analysis is becoming restricted' (Bion 1967a: 157). All such desires restrict the possibility of intuitive understanding.

Bion's technical recommendations are radical. To carry them out requires considerable discipline of an inner mental kind. What is required is nothing short of an inner emotional ascesis that can open out into new and unsuspected field of inquiry.

Bion spoke frequently of an analysand who had been referred to him as a 'very suitable' person for analysis. He describes the apparent acceptability to this patient of his various interpretations and then Bion's dawning realization that nothing was happening. He became aware that the patient was sealing himself up in his room so that he would not be disturbed in any way by others, and drinking his own urine. Finally he committed suicide.

One of Bion's preoccupations was with the question as to why certain people seem to understand and agree with the analyst's interpretations, yet remain untouched by analysis. Some may have suffered unchanged some somatic complaint, or else develop some psychosomatic illness. Others, like the man above, commit suicide. This indicated to him that something major was not being addressed in present-day psychoanalysis, and he addressed himself to trying to understand why.

He believed that it was highly likely that the continuity in the physical development of the foetus into post-natal life was paralleled by a similar continuity in mental life. He often quoted Freud's statement, 'There is much more continuity between intra-uterine life than the impressive caesura of the act of birth would have us believe' (Freud 1971e: 138). He imagined it possible that the foetal mind at some point was capable of becoming aware of unpleasant experiences, some of which might feel so intolerable to a mind not yet capable of dealing with this degree of pain that it might be capable of splitting off its awareness of it in order to get rid of it. This could also occur at the time of birth and this split-off aspect would remain hidden, the rest of the personality adapting apparently adequately to the demands of family and society until later in life when it might express itself in the form of psychotic or psychosomatic disturbance. In other words, that which was intolerable might re-emerge later in post-natal life, perhaps even under the influence of psychoanalysis.

Bion drew attention to the wording of Freud's statement, that the 'caesura would have us believe', as though the caesura actually ruled our thinking, making it difficult for us to see as continuous foetal mental life and post-natal mental life. In a similar way, we are accustomed to seeing body and mind as separate and this is another 'caesura' which is difficult to bridge.

The problem of communication between the two is explored in *A Memoir of the Future* in a conversation between two characters Body and Mind.

> *Mind:* You are borrowing [words] from me; do you get them through the diaphragm?
> *Body:* *They* penetrate *it.* But the meaning does not get through. Where did you get your pains from?
> *Mind:* Borrowed from the past. The meaning does not get through the barrier though. Funny – the meaning does not get through whether it is from you to me, or from me to you.
> *Body:* It is the meaning of pain that I am sending to you; the words get through – which I have not sent – but the meaning is lost.
>
> (Bion 1991: 433–4)

Bion uses the term 'soma-psychotic' to describe the other side of psychosomatic, the reversed perspective as it were. But there is a reluctance to bring them together, to see them from the other's point of view. This is the proto-mental system referred to initially in Bion's book on groups, where mental and physical are as yet undifferentiated. This is the area in which the foetus might experience her intolerable feelings, and be capable, even at a very immature foetal age, to split off that part of herself that is experiencing intolerable sensations/feelings and thus be freed of them. At birth the baby is already incomplete but is of such intelligence that it isn't noticed.

Bion wonders if there is communication of thought or pre-thought in the body before it registers at conscious levels, say along the sympathetic or parasympathetic nervous systems or the glandular system, particularly as the adrenaline produced by the adrenal medulla has the effect of activating the organism, rendering it ready, at least for fight or flight. This would provide an explanation of that state in which a patient says he is afraid but does not know of what.

How would it be possible to communicate with this archaic split-off area where feelings are experienced so intensely and in an unmodified way; the sorts of feelings to which Bion gives the name thalamic pain or thalamic fear, to indicate that it is unmodified by higher levels in the nervous system, and may therefore be of an unimaginable quality? Bion is exercised by the possibility of making contact with these archaic and somato-psychic areas which have not yet been able to penetrate to conscious levels.

In his lecture on 'Making the best of a bad job', Bion asks why so much more emphasis and validity is placed on the waking state as opposed to the dreaming-sleeping state. We talk about the dream-work, which is how the dream is constructed, including from waking elements; what about the wake-work by which, in the process of waking, the dream elements are dismissed as 'only a dream'?

> Why is the state of mind of being awake, conscious, logical, regarded as having 'our wits about us', but only if it is half our wits? How awful when you find a maggot in your apple! Not so awful as finding half a maggot in your apple. So we find that only having half our wits about us is a discovery that is most disturbing. It is one reason why there is a division of opinion as to whether to have all our wits about us, or to get back to having only one half – the wakeful, conscious, rational, logical.
>
> (Bion 1987: 254)

Bion's later writings reveal his preoccupation with our massive reluctance to confront reality and the ways in which we might be able to contact it. He points out that certain expressions using swear-words contain a primitive vitality as though contact is made with an archaic reality. Within the working-class culture in London it is well known that if one man points his finger accusingly at another and says 'You cunt' it will immediately start a fight.

Bion was very aware in his latter years that psychoanalysis was not effecting change in patients. He was very aware of those patients who looked as though they had changed; those who had put on the clothing of an analysed person but remained unchanged within. In particular he was conscious of those patients who subtly copied the analyst, took on his words, outlook and attitude, but in whom there was no change within. In other words there was an absence of alpha function and the articulations of the patient were an evacuation of beta elements. He tried to probe into this problem and his investigations into foetal life were one of his attempts to do so. The problem, however, remains unsolved.

Chapter 15

Ultimate reality, the mystic and the Establishment

But don't you think it pathetic that when Science and its brood of astronomers leads unmistakably to the discovery of our insignificance in contrast with those gigantic forces – novae, super novae, black holes and the rest – someone is sure to apply a mental first-aid dressing and hurl us back into the downy comfort of ignorance. Doesn't that depress you?

(Bion 1991: 573)

There are three axes which intersect and interpenetrate in Bion's thinking. They are ultimate reality, the difference between sensuous and psychic reality, and the way an individual comes to knowledge.

As we have pointed out in Chapter 1, many analysts shy away from Bion's concept of O, which he defines as being equivalent to ultimate reality, godhead, the truth, the infinite or the thing-in-itself. We believe that Bion did not start off with such a concept, but instead came to it through reflecting upon his clinical experience. After patiently waiting and observing, light dawned and he saw something, understood something – but what is the *something*? Even those who deplore what they feel is a quasi-religious formula use the same language when describing clinical insight. 'It had been there all along but suddenly I saw it,' says one analyst; or: 'Then at last I saw it, five years into the analysis', or a patient says, 'I have known Rob's attitude from the time I first met him but it is only now that I am aware of it.' What is the *it*? In the first case it is a grief that the patient is unable to bear, in the second it is the patient's sadism and in the third it is the patient's unhappiness. All these are psychic realities. You cannot see grief, touch it or smell it. The word 'grief' describes a psychic phenomenon. The tears and black clothes at a funeral signify grief but they are not it. There was once a funeral where the widow wore a blue trouser suit and the priest white vestments – in this case the grief was present but denied. In such a case it might take more time to discern the reality. In different cultures the signs of psychic realities are different. The tears and black clothes are what we see. This is what Bion describes as the sensuous, that is, it is discernible through the senses. Psychic reality is not discernible in that way. Similarly sadism and unhappiness cannot be seen. You cannot know psychic reality; you *become* it. The Spanish mystic St John of the Cross used the term *connaturality* and explained it thus. He said that a log of wood when thrown into the fire is cold; it then heats up and bursts into flames when it has reached the same heat as the fire. We think this is another way of expressing what Bion said:

> the analytic situation itself, and then the psycho-analytic occupation or task itself, are bound to stimulate primitive and basic feeling in analyst and analysand . . . these fundamental characteristics, love, hate, dread, are sharpened to a point where the participating pair may feel them to be almost unbearable.
>
> (Bion 1970: 66)

Why, though, does Bion take the matter further and say that what is emerging is not just different psychic realities but O, ultimate reality? Each time the analyst intuits the grief or the sadism he says, 'That's what it is.' In other words that's what makes the behaviour meaningful. He may say, 'It looks as though he does not care about the death of his loved one but the truth is, he is full of grief.' There is a judgement therefore that 'The truth is that grief is present.' There is a judgement as to what is true. The question then is: 'Does what is true correspond to a unity, a comprehensive reality?' Bion's answer to this has to be that it does.

When we say that the grief or sadism is truly present we mean that we confer value upon it; it is not just sham. So truth is that quality in things whereby they command our respect, as opposed to sham, which does not. What emerges in psychoanalysis is that which has true value as opposed to a deceptive appearance. So O is the term Bion designates for the truth; it is also ultimate in nature as it is not contingent on anything else.

On reading this, some may say that it is philosophical and is not relevant to psychoanalysis, but Bion's concern with psychoanalytic objects demands philosophical reflection. It is germane to his thinking that the human sciences are concerned with a unified reality and that they are carved up into different subjects – economics, sociology, psychology, anthropology – in order that detailed aspects can be studied separately, but that there is one reality which the thinker is trying to penetrate. Bion was profoundly concerned with what occurred in the consulting-room, but it was always a window into the whole human phenomenon. It is too restrictive to call Karl Marx an economist because he was also a psychologist and philosopher; it is too restrictive to call Darwin a biologist because he was also a geologist, palaeontologist, entomologist and philosopher; it is too restrictive to call Freud a neurologist because he was also a psychologist, social psychologist and philosopher. So with Bion it is too restrictive to call him a psychoanalyst because he was also a social psychologist, a biologist and philosopher. All these men were thinkers whose point of departure was in one discipline but whose thinking spread out to encompass humankind in several dimensions. To understand psychoanalysis it is necessary to go out in thought to those other dimensions and then return enriched to the point of departure before going out into the expanses again.

Bion is committed to the view that there is an absolute truth which can never be known directly. He says, 'The religious mystics have probably approximated most closely to expression of experience of it' (Bion 1970: 30). This ultimate reality is the psychoanalytic object *par excellence* of which others are only derivatives. This lies at the heart of Bion's thinking. The mystics, as he says, have probably approximated most closely to an experience of this ultimate reality. His approach then is to approximate as closely as possible to the mystics. He focuses attention on those defences we put up against entering such an experience.

Mysticism tends to be viewed pejoratively by those with a scientific attitude. Essentially mysticism is the record of the experiences of those who claim to have had close, even if not direct, contact with ultimate reality. True mystics always emphasize that this contact is not sensual but psychic. The question of whether these experiences are to be trusted can only be answered by scientific exploration. It is a prejudice to dismiss automatically all such experiences. The field of investigation is made more difficult by the fact that there have been many impostors, and even genuine mystical experiences are often clothed in language typifying the religiosity of the age, which is sometimes sentimental. Therefore there are many difficulties in trying to reach the experience itself. However, the scientific attitude is one that is open to the possibility of these special experiences and is able to examine them.

The inference is that Bion is open to believing in these experiences and that our task is to try to come as close to such an experience as is possible. However, the pathway by which such an experience becomes possible is through the close relationship with another. Psychoanalysis is the investigation of such a relationship and it attempts to open both partners to the mystical experience. Bion concentrates his focus on those elements that block the two individuals from that experience. The conclusion is unavoidable: that Bion's thinking is geared to facilitating mystical experience.

To the question 'How is the analyst to penetrate through the sensuous to the psychic reality?', Bion's answer is that he waits until a pattern begins to emerge and than he *intuits* the psychic reality.

The liar and lying is another topic which is closely associated with O. When the truth emerges it does not matter whether it is uttered through the analyst or the patient, a child or an adult, the Archbishop of Canterbury or Saddam Hussein, Stalin or Churchill, a Kleinian or a Kohutian. When we look at some of the marvellous statues that adorn our mediaeval cathedrals we do not know the sculptors who created them: they remain anonymous. Anonymity was part of the culture in that age, whereas in contemporary times, where the cult of the individual predominates, the creator is glorified; frequently this exaltation becomes the goal of the endeavour. The truth may need a mouthpiece but it can be anonymous. However a lie, whose purpose is to protect *amour-propre*, is inconceivable without a self-glorifying individual who needs an audience to prop him or her up. Bion's attitude to truth was similar to that of the Buddha, who said on his deathbed that his teachings should not be believed because he taught them but should instead be tested against experience. The individual's role is to be the vehicle of truth. Very often we do not hear the truth because it is spoken by someone we dislike. Unprejudiced openness to truth is a very difficult attitude to achieve.

Epilogue

One of the most difficult things when writing about psychoanalysis is that we use a word which means one thing for one reader and another for another. Kleinians, for instance, are very alert to the destructive forces in the personality. A Kleinian will frequently see the destructive force where an analyst from another school will not be aware of it. So as not to be polemical let us call that 'other school' the 'Optimistic School', to stand for any analyst who is unaware of those destructive forces which would usually be noted by the Kleinian. We would have to conjecture that the Optimist Analyst is blind to these destructive forces. The Optimist Analyst may then select those messages that are optimistically flavoured and reject those that have tones of destructiveness in them. We say this in order to introduce what we might call a note of hopefulness in Bion, but it is a hopefulness that he finds lodged in perversion, in malice even, and in hallucinations or delusions. In any of these, says Bion, there may be the seeds of a fruitful idea. While not blind to the perversion, the malice, the hallucination or the delusion, he was able to see the plant growing in the dung-heap.

Let us start with perversion. The very word 'perversion' means that there is something which has become perverted. We presume that this *something* is real and also good. 'Perverted' suggests that it is damaging in some way to the development of the personality and the individual's creative capacity, but that if *it*, the *something*, had not been perverted, it would have been beneficial to the personality. It is therefore necessary to look for the *something* of which the perversion is a skewed representation. A woman derived great pleasure from watching a man urinating and would have to make sure she observed this as frequently as possible.

She was a copy editor in a publishing company but had a great desire to write her own books. However, despite considerable literary talent, she was trapped in a mode of self-abasement and so remained a copy editor. The desire to write her own books, which in itself represented a desire for self-fulfilment, was symbolized in a man urinating. At the time when she had taken the job in the publishing company she had been offered to collaborate with someone in the writing of a play. She regretted bitterly that she had not done this, and to think that fifteen years had passed when she might by now have succeeded in being a prominent writer was painful in the extreme. She could not now fulfil her desire to write books without experiencing these painful regrets. In the perversion the desire was pleasurable, with its painful elements banished from awareness. However, in the perversion there was also the seed of a healthy desire which could be isolated from its sexual context over time in analysis.

What is true of a perversion is also true of a delusion, an hallucination and even of flagrant madness. We shall not give examples from all of these but take just one historical instance: that of Columbus. Christopher Columbus was enormously grandiose. He hung around the court of Isabella of Spain for eight years hassling her to finance his dream of an expedition – the sea-route to India – and when eventually she offered him a few ships, some financial assistance and her gracious favour and protection he demanded that he be Viceroy and Governor-General over all islands and continents that he might discover and occupy for Spain; that he be made Admiral of the World-Sea; that he be given a tenth part of all treasures found in the lands under his authority; that he have exclusive ownership of one-eighth of the lands to be discovered and conquered and that all these rights and titles be inherited by his successors. At first his demands were dismissed as outrageous and crazy, but he won through and the King and Queen agreed to all he requested. Earlier a royal commission cross-examined his proposals, proclaiming that his beliefs had no foundation. He had no rational argument to advance against them. All he had was an inner image of the sea-route to India and his own rock-like conviction. A psychiatrist examining him today would say he was deluded but that in that delusion was a truth: that setting out westwards by sea from the coast of Spain he would reach land; not the land of India, which he believed he had reached, but America. Again he was deluded, but there was a truth in the delusion and, interestingly, Isabella, the Queen, had an intuition that this was so: that amidst all this madness there was a grain of truth.

It is this grain of truth, this germ of a creative idea, that Bion believed was often encased within the madness. He said that in the psychotic process the variable becomes solidified into a constant. In the rigid idea is the flexible imaginative dawn of discovery, hidden in a rigid exterior.

In different chapters we have stressed the significance of O. O is the truth which can be known through the medium of science, religion or art. Different facets of O are known through these different media. When O emerges in the psychoanalytic process, contact is made with that ultimate reality which illuminates the sciences, religion and art. Bion made contact with O through the medium of psychoanalysis, but his ultimate concern was with O and not the vehicle through which it was approached. His concern went deep into the sinews of existence. What George Eliot says of her character Lydgate in *Middlemarch* could well have been said about Bion:

> He for his part had tossed away all cheap inventions where ignorance finds itself able and at ease: he was enamoured of that arduous invention which is the very eye of research, provisionally framing its object and correcting it to more and more exactness of relation; he wanted to pierce the obscurity of those minute processes which prepare human misery and joy, those invisible thoroughfares which are the first lurking-places of anguish, mania, and crime, that delicate poise and transition which determine the growth of happy or unhappy consciousness.
>
> (Eliot 1973: 194)

Bion looked through a microscope into the subtlest signals and also through a telescope to look into our distant past. This is probably what he is most concerned with in his last, enigmatic work, *A Memoir of the Future*.

A Memoir of the Future is a novel in which Bion expresses his theories and ideas in a form different from the scientific discourse of his other works. As a character in the book says, 'I was compelled to seek asylum in fiction. Disguised as fiction the truth occasionally slipped through' (Bion 1991: 302). It is his own *Aeneid*. It is his attempt to convey his ideas not only to psychoanalysts but also to a wider audience who might be receptive.

Bion sees the mind as being extremely limited in its ability to comprehend reality. He follows the Platonic concept of thoughts existing without the necessity of a thinker. Once a thinker is assumed to be essential, immediate restrictions are imposed, such as the polarization of truth and falsehood, a moral sense and time, with its inherent ideas of past and future, space and causality.

There is an inherent difficulty in believing or even imagining that there is a vast world of thoughts without a thinker which may exist free of the constraints of our normal rational thinking processes. This mind that 'spans too inadequate a spectrum of reality' (Bion 1991: 130) therefore is unable to discern the underlying patterns of phenomena concealed in this formless infinite. Perhaps these underlying patterns can only be hinted at in art, music, poetry. In psychoanalysis too, the various theories, of sexuality, aggression, rivalry, Oedipus complex, are not significant in themselves but rather are surface manifestations of an underlying configuration.

Contact with this non-sensuous and vast domain of thoughts may produce an experience so intense that it cannot be tolerated. Various defence mechanisms are immediately brought into play to provide an armour against any further awareness of this non-sensuous and unlimited domain. Mythology provides many examples of prohibitions against expanding knowledge: Adam and Eve, with God forbidding and punishing the pursuit of knowledge; Oedipus, who punishes himself when he discovers the truth; Herod's edict for the murder of all baby boys.

The book is concerned with the constraints we place on our own minds as soon as there is a threatened contact with the non-sensuous world of thought, because the pain, not sensuously apprehensible, is felt to be intolerable.

Our minds are so dominated by sensory phenomena that it is difficult for us to apprehend the non-sensuous reality. The visual image, for example, so dominates our thinking that it limits our ability to grasp this psychic reality. We need to be freed from this, in a manner analogous to the way in which the discovery of the Cartesian co-ordinates freed mathematics from the limitation of visual geometrical form, by revealing functions, the relationship between variables. Our very structuring of reality by the concepts of time, space and causality limits what we can understand.

Intolerance of the unknown and our need to snatch at something that 'explains' it smothers the opportunity of coming to the truth. People sometimes feel they think they are going to break down if the seed of truth is in danger of hatching out. We may take refuge in a tough prison of sanity and become like everyone else. We are restricted by the human mind that clings to an ideal, for example God; in such a case the variable is then substituted by a constant.

The Dawn of Oblivion, the third book in Bion's *A Memoir of the Future*, (1991), is an account of how a potentially open and aware mind learns the techniques of becoming oblivious to this greater reality and quickly learns to conform to the rigidities inherent in a complacent belief in man-made logic, laws and the restrictive framework of space and time. The book is an account of a journey from birth to death overwhelmed by pre-mature knowledge, experience, glory and self-intoxicating satisfaction. Ideas become rigid like an exoskeleton or a psychical osteo-arthritis with crippled articulations. By these means, the vitality is squeezed out of existence. The rigidity manifests itself in institutions which, with their rules, crush the life out of the very reason for their foundation. The individual becomes virtually a robot or else fights back. This is analogous to the foetus at term which might feel itself so compressed by the restricting uterus that it initiates the birth process.

Similarly in psychic life, the countless crushing forces might evoke a counter-reaction or rebellion, a breaking out of this imprisonment. It may be that the so-called 'mental breakdown' is a manifestation of breaking out. The breaking out or breaking through is not likely to be comfortable for the individual or for those close to him or her: family, friends and acquaintances.

The primitive is within us, the primaeval chaos. We continue to carry it with us just as we carry some of our original liquid environment in the form of the mucous membranes that line our alimentary and respiratory tracts, and the wet lining of the eyes and reproductive systems. This very wetness enables us to smell and to see and to reproduce. An excess of liquid, however, stops us from seeing and smelling.

The primitive brings vitality and is expressed in the primitive language of our swear-words. Reality is not civilized or polite, reasonable or considerate of our feelings and ideas. Nursery rhymes express the primitive vitality. The archaic chord is struck and vitality is released. This chord might penetrate the barriers and screens that obscure.

Divisions such as body and mind, or individuals, or days, hours and minutes, create a barrier, a screen or caesura between these parts which is difficult to bridge.

To register the primitive meaning, the vibrations from this ultimate reality, the equivalent of a sufficiently robust screen is necessary, but it must not be such that it will destroy the meaning either by denying it or by apparently accepting it with an 'I know'. It is this 'Yes, I know' response that is lethal to any attempt to explore, whether in psychoanalysis or in any other area. This basic assumption response is so often seen in a group; the 'We know best' that kills originality.

Bion is directing attention to the universal restriction of thinking, the ways in which it is manifested, and the anxiety associated with its removal. These resistances and fears are revealed in the analytic process.

This greater reality may reach us through the primitive precursors of the sensory apparatus – some 'vibration' may travel through fluid to reach the optic or auditory pits. It may not be registered in the usual way but perhaps more like an auditory or visual hallucination; in which case there is an immediate tendency to dismiss it as 'nonsense'. The solution to this is to observe the facts, no matter how repetitive they may appear to be, until a pattern begins to emerge. This was the advice of Charcot which Freud followed.

But if a pattern begins to emerge, it may be frightening, revealing brutality, greed, mindless destructiveness and cannibalistic impulses, so that the wish to continue the search is frozen at its source. We then quickly obliterate our awareness and sink back into our omniscient self-complacency.

Bion encouraged us to leave go of psychological comfort, venture forth into the unknown and risk the terror.

Chronology

1897	Born, 8 September, in Muttra in the United Provinces of India, where his father was an irrigation engineer.
1905–15	Bishop's Stortford College.
1916–18	Served with the Royal Tank Regiment. Awarded the Distinguished Service Order and Légion d'Honneur (Chevalier) and mentioned in Dispatches.
1919–21	Queen's College, Oxford.
1924–30	University College Hospital, London, where he was awarded the Gold Medal for Surgery.
1933–39	Secretary to the Medical Section of the British Psychological Society.
1940–45	Psychiatrist, Davy Hulme Military Hospital and Chester Military Hospital. Officer in charge, Northfield Military Hospital training wing. Senior Psychiatrist, War Office Selection Board.
1945–6	Chairman of the Executive Committee, Tavistock Clinic, London.
1946	Chairman of the Medical Section of the British Psychological Society.
1956–62	Director, London Clinic of Psycho-Analysis.
1962–65	President, British Psycho-Analytical Society.
1966–68	Member, Training Committee, British Psycho-Analytical Society. Chairman, Publications Committee, British Psycho-Analytical Society. Chairman, Melanie Klein Trust, British Psycho-Analytical Society.
1968	Moved to California to teach.

1968–79   Travelled widely in South America and Europe, lecturing and supervising.

1978   Honorary Member, Los Angeles Psycho-Analytic Society.

1979   Honorary fellow, A.K. Rice Institute.

Died, 8 November, in the John Radcliffe Hospital, Oxford, of acute myeloid leukemia.

Publications by Wilfred Bion

1940   'The war of nerves', in E. Miller and H. Crichton-Miller (eds), *The Neuroses in War*, London: Macmillan.

1943   'Intra-group tensions in therapy: their study as the task of the group', *The Lancet*, 27 November.

1946   'The leaderless group project', *Bulletin of the Menninger Clinic*, 10 (May).

1948   'Psychiatry at a time of crisis', *British Journal of Medical Psychology* 21.

1948–51   *Experiences in Groups, Human Relations, I–IV*; subsequently London: Tavistock Publications [see 1961 below].

1950   'The imaginary twin', presented to the British Psycho-Analytical Society (November) [Bion's membership paper]; *International Journal of Psycho-Analysis* (1955) and in *Second Thoughts* [see 1967 below].

1952   'Group dynamics: a review', *International Journal of Psycho-Analysis* 33; also in Melanie Klein, Paula Heimann and E. Money-Kyrle (eds), *New Directions in Psycho-Analysis* [see 1955 below] and in *Experiences in Groups* [see 1961 below].

1953   'Notes on the theory of schizophrenia', presented at the Eighteenth International Psycho-Analytic Congress; also in *International Journal of Psycho-Analysis* 35 (1954); also in *Second Thoughts* [see 1967a below].

1955   'Language and the schizophrenic patient', in Melanie Klein, Paula Heimann and E. Money-Kyrle (eds), *New Directions in Psycho-Analysis*, London: Tavistock Publications.

1956   'Development of schizophrenic thought', *International Journal of Psycho-Analysis* 37 (1956); also in *Second Thoughts* [see 1967a below].

1957a   'Differentiation of the psychotic from the non-psychotic personalities', *International Journal of Psycho-Analysis* 38 (1957); also in *Second Thoughts* [see 1967a below].

1957b   'On arrogance', presented at the Twentieth International Psycho-Analytic Congress, Paris; also in *International Journal of Psycho-Analysis* 39 (1958) and in *Second Thoughts* [see 1967a below].

1958 'On hallucination', *International Journal of Psycho-Analysis* 39 (1958); also in *Second Thoughts* [see 1967a below].

1959 'Attacks on linking', *International Journal of Psycho-Analysis*, 40; also in *Second Thoughts* [see 1967a below].

1961 *Experiences in Groups*, London: Tavistock Publications.

1962a 'A theory of thinking', *International Journal of Psycho-Analysis*, 53; also in *Second Thoughts* [see 1967a below].

1962b *Learning from Experience*, London: William Heinemann, Medical Books; reprinted London: Karnac Books, 1984; also in *Seven Servants* [see 1977a below].

1963 *Elements of Psycho-Analysis*, London: William Heinemann, Medical Books; reprinted London: Karnac Books, 1984; also in *Seven Servants* [see 1977a below].

1965 *Transformations*, London: William Heinemann, Medical Books; reprinted London: Karnac Books, 1984; also in *Seven Servants* [see 1977a below].

1966 'Catastrophic change', *Bulletin 5*, British Psycho-Analytical Society; also in *Attention and Interpretation* (Chapter 12) [see 1970 below].

1967a *Second Thoughts*, London: William Heinemann, Medical Books [contains the papers indicated above, together with a 'Commentary'].

1967b 'Notes on memory and desire', *The Psychoanalytic Forum* 2(3) (Los Angeles, California).

1970 *Attention and Interpretation*, London: Tavistock Publications; reprinted London: Karnac Books, 1984; also in *Seven Servants*, [see 1977a below].

1973 *Brazilian Lectures, 1*, Rio de Janeiro: Imago Editora; also in *Brazilian Lectures* [see 1990 below].

1974 *Brazilian Lectures, 2*, Rio de Janeiro: Imago Editora; also in *Brazilian Lectures* [see 1990 below].

1975 *A Memoir of the Future, Book One: The Dream*, Rio de Janeiro: Imago Editora; also in *A Memoir of the Future* [see 1991 below].

1976a 'Emotional turbulence', paper given at the International Conference on Borderline Disorders, Topeka, Kansas (March); published in the book of the conference (New York: International Universities Press, 1977); also in *Clinical Seminars and Four Papers* [see 1987 below].

1976b 'On a quotation from Freud', paper given at the International Conference on Borderline Disorders, Topeka, Kansas (March); published in the book of the conference (New York: International Universities Press, 1977); also in *Clinical Seminars and Four Papers* [see 1987 below].

1976c 'Evidence', *Bulletin 8*, British Psycho-Analytical Society; also in *Clinical Seminars and Four Papers* [see 1987 below].

1976d Interview with Anthony G. Banet Jr, published in *Groups and Organization Studies*, I(3).

1977a   *Seven Servants*, New York: Jason Aronson [contains the four books indicated above].

1977b   *A Memoir of the Future, Book Two: The Past Presented*, Rio de Janeiro: Imago Editora; also in *A Memoir of the Future*, [see 1990 below].

1977c   *Two Papers: The Grid and Caesura* [originally presented as talks to the Los Angeles Psycho-Analytic Society, in 1971 and 1975, respectively] Rio de Janeiro: Imago Editora; new edition London: Karnac Books, 1989

1978   *Four Discussions with W.R. Bion*, Strath Tay, Perthshire: Clunie Press.

1979a   *A Memoir of the Future, Book Three: The Dawn of Oblivion*, Strath Tay, Perthshire: Clunie Press; also in *A Memoir of the Future* [see 1990 below].

1979b   'Making the best of a bad job', *Bulletin 20*, British Psycho-Analytical Society; also in *Clinical Seminars and Four Papers* [see 1987 below].

1980   *Bion in New York and São Paulo*, Strath Tay, Perthshire: Clunie Press.

1981   *A Key to a Memoir of the Future*, Strath Tay, Perthshire: Clunie Press; also in *A Memoir of the Future* [see 1990 below].

1982   *The Long Week-End – 1897–1919*, Abingdon: Fleetwood Press.

1985   *All My Sins Remembered and The Other Side of Genius*, Abingdon: Fleetwood Press.

1986   *Seminari Italiani*, Rome: Borla [published in Italian only].

1987   *Clinical Seminars and Four Papers*, Abingdon: Fleetwood Press.

1990   *Brazilian Lectures*, Karnac Books [a new one-volume edition of the two books listed above].

1991   *A Memoir of the Future*, London: Karnac Books [a new one-volume edition of the two books listed above].

1992   *Cogitations*, London: Karnac Books.

Bibliography

Blaedel, N. (1988) *Harmony and Unity: The Life of Niels Bohr*, Madison, WI: Science Tech Publishers.

Blake, W. (1972) 'Eternity', in *Blake: Complete Writings*, Oxford: Oxford University Press.

Bleandonu, G. (1994) *Wilfred Bion: His Life and Work, 1897–1979*. London: Free Association Books and New York: The Guilford Press.

Bonham Carter, V. (1965) *Churchill as I Knew Him*, London: The Reprint Society.

Casement, P. (1990) *Further Learning from the Patient*, London: Routledge.

Davies, P. (1984) *God and the New Physics*, London: Penguin.

Dostoevsky, F.M. (1978) *Crime and Punishment*, Harmondsworth: Penguin.

Eliot, G. (1973) *Middlemarch*, Harmondsworth: Penguin.

Fish, F.J. (1962) *Schizophrenia*, Bristol: John Wright & Sons.

Flavell, J.H. (1963) *The Developmental Psychology of Jean Piaget*, New York: Van Nostrand Reinhold.

Freud, S. (1971a) *Pre-Psycho-Analytic Publications and Unpublished Drafts: The Standard Edition of the Complete Psychological Works of Sigmund Freud, Vol. I*, London: Hogarth Press and the Institute of Psycho-Analysis; New York: Macmillan.

—— (1971b) *The Interpretation of Dreams and On Dreams: The Standard Edition of the Complete Psychological Works of Sigmund Freud, Vol. V*, London: Hogarth Press and the Institute of Psycho-Analysis; New York: Macmillan.

—— (1971c) *Five Lectures on Psycho-Analysis, Leonardo and Other Works: The Standard Edition of the Complete Psychological Works of Sigmund Freud, Vol. XI*, London: Hogarth Press and the Institute of Psycho-Analysis; New York: Macmillan.

—— (1971d) *The Ego and the Id and Other Works: The Standard Edition of the Complete Psychological Works of Sigmund Freud, Vol. XIX*, London: Hogarth Press and the Institute of Psycho-Analysis; New York: Macmillan.

—— (1971e) *An Autobiographical Study, Inhibitions, Symptoms and Anxiety, Lay Analysis and Other Works: The Standard Edition of the*

Complete Psychological Works of Sigmund Freud, Vol. XX, London: Hogarth Press and the Institute of Psycho-Analysis; New York: Macmillan.

Fromm, E. (1972) *Psychoanalysis and Religion*, New Haven, CT: Bantam Books–Yale University Press.

Grosskurth, P. (1985) *Melanie Klein: Her World and Her Work*, London: Hodder & Stoughton.

Hoffman, E. (1991) *Lost in Translation*, London: Minerva.

Hughes, T. (1982) 'The thought fox', in *Selected Poems*, London: Faber & Faber.

Huxley, A. (1980) *The Perennial Philosophy*, London: Chatto & Windus.

Kant, I. (1956) *Critique of Practical Reason*, Indianapolis and New York: Bobbs Merrill.

Koestler, A. (1975) *The Act of Creation*, London: Picador, Pan Books.

Lonergan, B. (1958) *Insight*, London: Darton, Longman & Todd.

Magagna, J. (1994) 'The eye turned inwards', in Luigia Cresti Scacciati (ed.) (1996) *Contrappunto*, Florence: Associazione Fiorentina di Psicoterapia Psicoanalitica.

Matte Bianco, I. (1975) *The Unconscious as Infinite Sets: An Essay in Bi-Logic*, London: Duckworth.

Murdoch, I. (1992) *Metaphysics as a Guide to Morals*, London: Allen Lane, Penguin.

Newman, J.H. (1876) *Parochial and Plain Sermons*, Vol. 5, London, Oxford and Cambridge: Rivingtons.

Orwell, G. (1972) *The Road to Wigan Pier*, Harmondsworth: Penguin.

Pines, M. (1987) 'Bion: a group-analytic appreciation', in *Group Analysis*, Vol. 20, Part III, pp. 25–62.

Poincaré, H. (1952) *Science and Method*, New York: Dover Publications.

Read, H. (1974) *A Concise History of Modern Painting*, London: Thames & Hudson.

Reeves, J.W. (1965) *Thinking about Thinking*, London: Secker & Warburg.

Russell, B. (1993) *Introduction to Mathematical Philosophy*, London: Routledge & Kegan Paul.

Schmandt-Besserat, D. (1992) *Before Writing: From Counting to Cuneiform*, Austin: University of Texas Press.

Solovyov, V. (1918) *The Justification of the Good*, London: Constable.

Vygotsky, L.S. (1975) *Thought and Language*, Cambridge, MA: MIT Press.

Weizsäcker, C.F.F. von (1973) Introduction to G. Krishna, *The Biological Basis of Religion and Genius*, London: Turnstone Press.

Whitehead, A.F. (1958) *An Introduction to Mathematics*, Oxford: Oxford University Press.

Index